THE

TRANSATLANTIC ECONOMY 2014

Annual Survey of Jobs, Trade and Investment
between the United States and Europe

DANIEL S. HAMILTON AND JOSEPH P. QUINLAN

CENTER FOR TRANSATLANTIC RELATIONS JOHNS HOPKINS UNIVERSITY
PAUL H. NITZE SCHOOL OF ADVANCED INTERNATIONAL STUDIES

Hamilton, Daniel S., and Quinlan, Joseph P.,
The Transatlantic Economy 2014: Annual Survey of Jobs, Trade and Investment between the United States and Europe

Washington, DC: Center for Transatlantic Relations, 2014.
© Center for Transatlantic Relations, 2014

Center for Transatlantic Relations
American Consortium on EU Studies
EU Center of Excellence Washington, DC
The Paul H. Nitze School of Advanced International Studies
The Johns Hopkins University
1717 Massachusetts Ave., NW, Suite 525
Washington, DC 20036
Tel: (202) 663-5880
Fax: (202) 663-5879
Email: transatlantic@jhu.edu
http://transatlantic.sais-jhu.edu
ISBN 978-0-9890294-2-1
ISBN 978-0-9890294-5-2

Table of Contents

Preface and Acknowledgements

This annual survey offers the most up-to-date picture of the dense economic relationship binding European countries to America's 50 states. The survey consists of two volumes. Volume One offers Headline Trends for the transatlantic economy, and updates with the latest facts and figures our basic framework for understanding the deeply integrated transatlantic economy via 'eight ties that bind.' Volume Two provides the most up-to-date information on European-sourced jobs, trade and investment with the 50 U.S. states, and U.S.-sourced jobs, trade and investment with the 28 member states of the European Union, as well as Norway, Switzerland and Turkey.

This annual survey complements our other writings in which we use both geographic and sectoral lenses to examine the deep integration of the transatlantic economy, and the role of the U.S. and Europe in the global economy, with particular focus on how globalization affects American and European consumers, workers, companies, and governments. In our other new publication, *Atlantic Rising: Changing Commercial Dynamics in the Atlantic Basin* (2014), we and fellow authors explore the new connections being forged among the four Atlantic continents in terms of energy, goods, services, and investment, and present a host of often counterintuitive conclusions.

We also are providing regular analyses of the Transatlantic Trade and Investment Partnership, or TTIP, currently being negotiated between the United States and the European Union via the Center's Transatlantic Partnership Forum.

We would like to thank Lisa Mendelow, James Medaglio, Andrew Vasylyuk and Dylan Meola for their assistance in producing this study.

We are grateful for generous support of our annual survey from the American Chamber of Commerce to the European Union and its member companies; and the Transatlantic Business Council and its member companies.

The views expressed here are our own, and do not necessarily represent those of any sponsor or institution. Other views and data sources have been cited, and are appreciated.

Daniel S. Hamilton
Joseph P. Quinlan

EXECUTIVE SUMMARY

» Despite continuing transatlantic economic turbulence, the U.S. and Europe remain each other's most important markets. No other commercial artery in the world is as integrated.

» The transatlantic economy generates $5 trillion in total commercial sales a year and employs up to 15 million workers in mutually "onshored" jobs on both sides of the Atlantic.

» Ties are particular thick in foreign direct investment, portfolio investment, banking claims, trade and affiliate sales in goods and services, mutual R&D investment, patent cooperation, technology flows, and sales of knowledge-intensive services.

» The transatlantic economy is the largest and wealthiest market in the world, accounting for over 50% of world GDP in terms of value and roughly 40% in terms of purchasing power.

» Europe accounts for 19.6% of world GDP and over one-quarter of global consumption. The EU is the world's largest exporting entity; the world's largest trader in goods and services; the top supplier of goods to developing countries; and the largest trading partner of each of the BRICs—Brazil, Russia, India, China. It is the largest provider and recipient of foreign direct investment among all world regions.

» The U.S. remains by a wide margin the most productive and wealthiest large economy in the world. It continues to attract more FDI than any other single national economy—$159 billion in 2013, greater than combined inflows to China and India ($155 billion) and nearly 11% of total global FDI inflows of $1.46 trillion.

» As globalization proceeds and emerging markets rise, however, transatlantic markets are shifting from a position of preeminence to one of predominance – still considerable, but less overwhelming than in the past.

» The nature and vibrancy of transatlantic economic activity in 2014 will turn on

  » whether the U.S. economy can break free from lingering recession and grow more than 3%;

  » whether Europe can avoid an economic relapse and build on its fragile recovery of 2013; and

  » whether U.S. and EU TTIP negotiators can demonstrate tangible progress toward reaching one of the most ambitious and far-reaching commercial agreements in history.

» Risks remain. U.S. banks are not overly exposed to either Greece or Portugal: outstanding U.S. loans/claims in Greece totaled just $11 billion and $3.8 billion in Portugal in late 2013. Yet U.S. financial institutions are quite heavily exposed to the UK, Italy, France and Germany, which in turn are highly leveraged to some of Europe's most financially stressed nations.

» There were some 37.4 million unemployed workers in Europe and the United States in November 2013, a staggering figure and an astounding waste of human potential.

The Importance of TTIP

» 2014 is a pivotal year for the Transatlantic Trade and Investment Partnership (TTIP).

» A transatlantic zero-tariff agreement could boost U.S. and EU exports each by 17%—about five times more than under the U.S.-Korea free trade agreement.

» Even greater gains would be realized through reductions in non-tariff barriers and aligning regulatory standards. Eliminating or harmonizing half of all non-tariff barriers on bilateral commerce would add 0.7% to the size of the EU's economy and 0.3% to America's economy by 2018. Such an effort would be 3 times more beneficial to the U.S. and EU economies than current offers on the negotiating table in the Doha Round. Even a 25% reduction in non-tariff barriers could lead to a $106 billion increase in combined EU and U.S. GDP.

» Eliminating barriers to services would have a substantial impact on jobs and growth, since most American and European jobs are in the services economy, and protected services sectors on both sides of the Atlantic account for about 20% of combined U.S.-EU GDP—more than the protected agricultural and manufacturing sectors combined. Removing services barriers would be equivalent to 50 years' worth of GATT and WTO liberalization of trade in goods.

» TTIP's global impact could be even more important than opening transatlantic commerce. Transatlantic alignment on basic standards and norms is likely to set the tone for high, WTO-plus global standards; failure will mean lowest-common-denominator standards set by others.

Transatlantic Investment: Still Driving the Transatlantic Economy

» Trade alone is a misleading benchmark of international commerce; mutual investment dwarfs trade and is the real backbone of the transatlantic economy. The U.S. and Europe are each other's primary source and destination for foreign direct investment.

» Together the U.S. and Europe accounted for only 25% of global exports and 31% of global imports in 2012. But together they accounted for 56.7% of the inward stock of foreign direct investment (FDI), and a whopping 71% of outward stock of FDI. Moreover, each partner has built up the great majority of that stock in the other economy. Mutual investment in the North Atlantic space is very large, dwarfs trade, and has become essential to U.S. and European jobs and prosperity.

» Foreign investment and affiliate sales drive transatlantic trade. 61% of U.S. imports from the EU consisted of intra-firm trade in 2011. That is much higher than U.S. intra-firm imports from Pacific Rim countries (37.2%) and South/Central America (37%), and well above the global average (48.3%). Percentages are notably high for Ireland (88.5%) and Germany (68.7%).

» Intra-firm trade also accounted for 32.3% of U.S. exports to Europe and nearly half of total U.S. exports to Belgium and the Netherlands, 34.9% of exports to Germany and 27.9% of exports to the UK.

The U.S. in Europe

» Over many decades no place in the world has attracted more U.S. FDI than Europe. Since the start of this century Europe has attracted 56% of total U.S. global investment. Thus far this decade Europe's global share of U.S. FDI has actually increased to 56.2% of the total, up from a 55.9% share over the 2000-09 period.

» U.S. FDI outflows to Europe rose by 6% in 2013, totaling an estimated $200 billion. Flows fell through the year but rebounded towards the end of the year.

» In the first nine months of 2013, U.S. FDI to Europe fell 6.7% from a year earlier. FDI flows to Germany and France fell sharply; flows were weak to the UK, Spain and other countries. Flows to Poland, Ireland and the Netherlands were strong.

» The Netherlands ($47.4 billion), the UK ($32.7 billion) and Ireland ($17.8 billion), the top three destinations for U.S. firms over the January-September 2013 period, accounted for just over 70% of U.S. investment to the EU; since 2000, they have accounted for 79% of the total U.S. FDI to the European Union. In the January-September 2013 period, flows to Ireland and the Netherlands rose 7% and 14.6%, respectively; flows to the UK dropped by over 21%.

» U.S. FDI flows between January-September 2013 to Germany declined 103% and were down 30% to France. However, sharp first quarter declines were followed by rebounding investments through the rest of the year.

» U.S. FDI flows soared 152% to Denmark and 103% to Poland in the first nine months of 2013. U.S. investment rose nearly 30% to Finland and 14.3% to the Czech Republic.

» U.S. FDI has not shifted *away* from Europe, but it is shifting *within* Europe. Denmark has attracted a greater share of U.S. FDI this decade (1.2%) than the two prior decades. U.S. investment in Poland and in Luxembourg has increased substantially. Ireland's share has jumped 2.4% this decade to 12.4% versus a share of 10% over 2000-09 and just 4.6% over the 1990s. The Netherlands' share this decade is 29.4%, while the UK's take is roughly 20% of the total.

» Conversely, Belgium's share has declined this decade, to 1.6%, down from 2.6% in the 1990s and 3.5% over the 2000-09 time frame. France's share amounts to just 1.4% this decade, down from 3.7% over 2000-09 and 6.2% over the 1990s. Germany's share dropped from 6.8% over the 1990s, to 5.2% last decade, to just 2.7% thus far this decade. Some of these figures need to be taken with a grain of salt, since some U.S. investment in countries neighboring Germany, for instance the Netherlands, Luxembourg or Belgium, finds its way ultimately to Germany.

» Italy, Spain and Switzerland have also experienced declines in U.S. investments as a share of the European total. Spain's share this decade has plummeted to just 0.3%.

» In 2013, however, U.S. FDI flows rose sharply to Italy and were slightly positive to Spain. U.S. disinvestment flows from Greece slowed to $2 million, but followed massive disinvestments from the country since 2009. U.S. firms also disinvested some $17 million from Portugal.

» Ireland is the number one export platform in the world for Corporate America. Between 2000 and 2011, U.S. affiliate exports from Ireland jumped almost five-fold to nearly $240 billion. U.S. affiliate exports from Ireland are 5 times larger than U.S. affiliate exports from China and 3.5 times larger than from Mexico.

» U.S. investment stock in central and eastern Europe has expanded greatly. U.S. investment stock in Poland rose from just $1 billion in 1995 to over $14 billion in 2012, on a par with U.S. investment stock in Russia and larger than America's investment position in Indonesia ($11.6 billion) one of Asia's most populous nations. U.S. investment stock in the Czech Republic was $6.4 billion in 2012, slightly greater than America's investment presence in the Philippines.

» Within Europe, America's top overseas market has shifted from the UK to the Netherlands. The UK has traditionally served as an export platform for U.S. affiliates to greater Europe, but the euro, the Single Market, and EU enlargement have all galvanized more U.S. firms to use the Netherlands as a key export platform and pan-regional distribution hub. The bulk of total U.S. foreign affiliate sales in the Netherlands are exports going to other EU members.

» China has accounted for just 1.2% of total global U.S. investment since the start of this century. U.S. investment in the Netherlands was more than 14 times larger; U.S. investment in the UK was more than 10 times larger; and U.S. investment in Ireland more than 6 times larger than U.S. investment in China.

» Since 2000 U.S. firms have invested more in the Netherlands ($513 billion) and the UK ($383 billion) alone than in South and Central America, the Middle East and Africa combined ($341 billion).

» U.S. cumulative investment in Brazil since 2000 ($52.6 billion) has been roughly one-quarter U.S. investment in Ireland.

» FDI in Russia since 2000 ($9 billion) has been less than in such smaller European countries as Norway ($22.9 billion) and Denmark ($14.7 billion).

» Since 2000 U.S. FDI in India ($27.7 billion) has been less than in Italy ($34.5 billion).

» On a historic cost basis, the U.S. investment position in Europe was 14 times larger than the BRICs and nearly 4 times larger than in all of Asia at the end of 2012.

» U.S. investment in the Netherlands alone is about 4 times larger, and U.S. investment in the UK 3 times larger, than U.S. investment in all of the BRICs.

» America's investment stakes in Ireland ($204 billion) were much greater than total U.S. capital sunk in South America ($171 billion).

» There is more U.S. investment in Germany ($121 billion) than in Mexico and all of Central America ($113 billion).

» U.S. investment in Switzerland ($130 billion) is more than double all of U.S. FDI in Africa ($61 billion).

» Of Corporate America's total foreign assets globally, roughly 60%—$13.2 trillion—was in Europe in 2012. Largest shares: the UK (22.5%, $5.1 trillion) and the Netherlands (nearly 9%, $2.0 trillion).

» America's asset base in Germany ($721 billion) in 2012 was over 50% larger than its asset base in all of South America.

» America's combined asset base in Poland, Hungary, and the Czech Republic (roughly $136 billion) was much larger than corporate America's assets in India (est. $100 billion).

» U.S. assets in Ireland topped $1 trillion in 2012, more than total U.S. assets in either Switzerland or France. Ireland accounted for 8.1% of total U.S. assets in Europe in 2012.

» Total output of U.S. foreign affiliates in Europe in 2012 ($760 billion) and of European affiliates in the U.S. ($500 billion) was greater than the output of such countries as the Netherlands, Turkey or Indonesia.

» U.S. affiliate output in Europe rose 6% in 2012 to total $760 billion, recovering to surpass the pre-crisis high of $660 billion in 2008.

» Aggregate output of U.S. affiliates globally reached nearly $1.6 trillion in 2012; Europe accounted for 48% of the total.

» The UK accounted for 22% of total U.S. affiliate output in Europe, followed by Ireland (13.7%) and Germany (13.3%).

» These 3 countries accounted for roughly half of total U.S. affiliate output in Europe in 2012, Ireland's share of U.S. foreign affiliate output has risen 2.74 times from 5% in 2000 to 13.7% in 2012. France's share of U.S. affiliate output, in contrast, dropped from 8.4% in 2010 to 7.7% in 2012.

» By sector, output is tilting to services (53%) over manufacturing (47%). Germany, the UK and Ireland accounted for roughly half of total U.S. affiliate manufacturing output in Europe.

» U.S. affiliates accounted for over 25% of Ireland's total output in 2012; 6% of the UK's output; 5.8% of Norway's output; 5% of Switzerland's output; and 4.9% of Belgium's total output.

» U.S. foreign affiliate output in Belgium in 2012 (roughly $25.5 billion) was more than 40% larger than U.S. foreign affiliate output in India (est. $18 billion).

» U.S. affiliate output in Poland totaled an estimated $12.6 billion in 2012. U.S. affiliates boosted their Polish output six-fold between 2000 and 2012.

» U.S. affiliate sales in Europe topped $3 trillion for the first time in 2012 and accounted for 48% of worldwide U.S. affiliate sales.

» Sales of U.S. affiliates in Europe in 2012 were roughly double comparable sales in the entire Asia/Pacific. Affiliate sales in the UK ($655 billion) alone were almost double sales in South America. Sales in Germany ($352 billion) were 80% larger than combined sales in Africa and the Middle East.

» While U.S. affiliate sales in China have soared over the past decade, they have done so from a low base, and still remain well below comparable sales in Europe. U.S. affiliate sales of $206 billion in China in 2011 were below those in Ireland ($320 billion), Switzerland ($304 billion) the Netherlands ($228 billion) or France ($220 billion).

» Combined U.S. foreign affiliate sales in Poland, Hungary and the Czech Republic, home to roughly 60 million people, surged roughly 270% between 2000 and 2011, rising from $21 billion to $77.6 billion, about one-third larger than affiliate sales in India, home to over 1.2 billion people.

» Europe remains the most profitable region of the world for U.S. companies. U.S. foreign affiliate income earned in Europe rose modestly in 2013 to an estimated $230 billion—a record high. Income declines were reported for the first nine months of 2013 in Greece (-144%), Italy (-65%), Germany (-63%), Spain (-25%), and France (-12%); and income increases in the United Kingdom (12.8%), Switzerland (8%), and Ireland (1.1%).

» Since 2000, Europe has accounted for over 57% of total U.S. foreign affiliate income.

» U.S. affiliate income from China and India together in 2011 ($10.4 billion) was only 15% of what U.S. affiliates earned in the Netherlands ($73 billion) and a fraction of U.S. affiliate earnings in the UK ($36 billion) or Ireland ($30 billion).

» In the first nine months of 2013, U.S. affiliate income from Europe—$172 billion—more was more than combined U.S. affiliate income from Latin America ($64 billion) and Asia ($56 billion).

» U.S. affiliate income in China ($7 billion) or Brazil ($5.7 billion), however, was well above affiliate income in Germany ($1.1 billion) or France ($2.2 billion).

» U.S. capital outflows to the EU15 totaled roughly $185 billion in 2013, a sharp rise from the previous year ($86 billion). A large part of this gain was related to U.S. investors allocating more capital towards European bonds and equities in anticipation of Europe's economic rebound.

Europe in the U.S.

» FDI inflows from Europe to the United States have declined in past years. European FDI to the U.S. plunged 37% in the first nine months of 2013 and declined 17.7% in 2012. For the year, we estimate that Europe's FDI investment in the U.S. totaled roughly $80 billion, one of the weakest levels in years. This follows investment inflows of $105 billion in 2012 and $128 billion in 2011.

» A massive one-off disinvestment from Belgium of -$13.3 billion in the first three quarters of 2013 distorted total FDI inflows to the U.S. Excluding Belgium, FDI inflows from Europe to the U.S. for this period dropped by 7.6%, rather than 37%.

» FDI inflows plunged 118% from Germany; 108% from Sweden; 66% from France; 30% from the Netherlands, and 10% from the UK.

» The downturn was less about difficult economic conditions in the United States, and more about European firms (financials) sending capital back home or downsizing their global operations in the face of weakening global demand and recessionary conditions in Europe.

» Europe accounted for 71% of the $2.65 trillion invested in the United States in 2012 on a historic cost basis. The bulk of the capital was sunk by British firms (with total UK stock amounting to $487 billion), the Netherlands ($275 billion), France ($209 billion), Switzerland ($204 billion) and Germany ($199 billion).

» Europe's investment flows to the United States in 2012 were some four times larger than comparable flows to China.

» In 2012 total assets of European affiliates in the U.S. were an estimated $8.7 trillion. UK firms held $2.2 trillion, followed by German firms ($1.5 trillion), Swiss (roughly $1.4 trillion), French ($1.2 trillion) and Dutch firms ($1 trillion).

» The U.S. remains the most important market in the world in terms of earnings for many European multinationals. European affiliates earned an estimated $119 billion in the U.S. in 2013—sizable, but down 4.8% from 2012 record levels.

» European affiliate output in the U.S. rose by nearly 6.5% in 2012, totaling over $ billion, a record high.

» The output of British firms in the U.S. in 2012 reached nearly $128 billion—more than a quarter of the European total. German affiliate output totaled $87 billion, or about 18% of the total. French affiliate output ($64 billion) accounted for 13% of the total.

» Beyond European affiliates, only Japan and Canada have any real economic presence in the U.S.—Japanese affiliate output totaled $92 billion in 2011, well below UK output and roughly similar to German affiliate output; Canadian affiliate output totaled $65 billion, on a par with French affiliate output.

» Overall, foreign affiliates contributed nearly $775 billion to U.S. aggregate production in 2012, with European affiliates accounting for roughly two-thirds of the total.

» Affiliate sales, not trade, are the primary means by which European firms deliver goods and services to U.S. consumers. In 2012 European affiliate sales in the U.S. ($2.2 trillion) were more than triple U.S. imports from Europe ($655 billion). Affiliate sales rose roughly 6% in 2012.

» Sales by British affiliates in the U.S. totaled an estimated $521 billion in 2012, followed by German affiliate sales ($411 billion) and those by Dutch affiliates ($374 billion).

» While Europe remains a key provider of capital to the United States, portfolio flows from Europe to the United States declined sharply in 2013. EU15 purchases of U.S. securities assets fell 16%; purchases of U.S. Treasuries plunged 58%; and purchases of U.S. equities declined 33% in the first eleven months of 2013 versus the same period a year earlier. Total portfolio inflows from the EU15 to the U.S. amounted to roughly $115 billion in 2013, one of the lowest levels since the early 1990s.

» This plunge reflects the credit and capital stress of Europe, with more investors—private and public—needing to raise capital at home to cover their expenses and credit obligations. The downturn also reflects, in part, investor unease with how the U.S. government conducts business, with the government shutdown in late 2013 leading to large selling of U.S. securities among foreigners.

» China, Japan and Europe hold roughly equal shares of U.S. Treasuries. As of November 2013, China held $1.3 trillion in U.S. Treasuries, or 23% of the total; Japan and Europe each held close to $1.2 trillion, or 21% of the total. OPEC's share was around 4%.

Transatlantic Trade

» U.S.-EU merchandise trade totaled an estimated $787 billion in 2013, more than double the level at the start of the new century.

» The U.S. 2013 merchandise trade deficit with the EU surged to $125 billion in 2013, 8% larger than in 2012 and more than double the deficit in 2009.

» Germany accounted for nearly half the deficit; America's $67 billion trade deficit with Germany rose 12.2% from 2012. U.S. exports to Germany fell 2.8%, to $47.4 billion, while imports rose 5.5%, to $114.6 billion.

» U.S. exports posted gains to Belgium (7.7%), the Netherlands (5%), France (3.8%), Italy (2.6%) and a host of smaller nations in 2013. The largest U.S. export declines were reported with Sweden (-17.9%), the UK (-13.7%), and Ireland (-10.4%). The U.S. posted large trade deficits with France ($13.3 billion), Ireland ($25 billion), Italy ($22.1 billion), and the UK ($5.3 billion).

» In contrast, the U.S. consistently records services trade surpluses with Europe—nearly $67 billion in 2012 and $51 billion in the first nine months of 2013.

» U.S. exports to Europe by state varied in 2013; Hawaii, Kentucky and New Mexico posted large year-over-year gains, while Utah, Nevada and Florida posted large declines. Exports from Texas were down nearly 4% but in the context of soaring energy exports from Texas to Europe over the past few years, with petroleum and coal exports topping $11 billion in 2012. That is more than ten times the level of exports in 2005 and reflects Texas' surging energy production.

» 45 of 50 U.S. states export more to Europe than to China, and by a wide margin in many cases. In the first nine months of 2013 Florida, New Jersey and Rhode Island each exported roughly 8 times more to Europe than to China; Connecticut 7 times more; Indiana and West Virginia 6 times more; New York, Maryland, Delaware, Nevada and Wyoming 5 times more; and Iowa, Kentucky, Massachusetts, New Hampshire over 4 times more. Texas, the leading U.S. state exporter to Europe, sent more than 3 times as many goods to Europe than to China as did 7 other states, including Arizona and New Mexico, Ohio, Pennsylvania and Virginia. The Pacific coast state of California exported twice as much to Europe as to China, as did 14 other states ranging from Illinois, Michigan and Colorado to North Carolina, Wisconsin and Tennessee.

» Germany was the top European export market for 18 U.S. states in 2012. The UK was the top European export market for 11 states. The Netherlands and Belgium were each the top European destination for 7 states.

» Global Value Chains, which render a country's exports essentially the product of many intermediate imports assembled in many other countries, are changing traditional understanding of the patterns and structure of international trade. Under WTO/OECD "value-added" calculations, the U.S. in 2009 was the major customer and supplier for Germany, the UK, France and Italy. Germany followed only Canada as the most important export market for the United States, ahead of Mexico and China.

Services: The Sleeping Giant of the Transatlantic Economy

» The U.S. and Europe are the two leading services economies in the world. The U.S. is the largest single country trader in services, while the EU is the largest trader in services among all world regions. The U.S. and EU are each other's most important commercial partners and major growth markets when it comes to services trade and investment. Moreover, deep transatlantic connections in services industries, provided by mutual investment flows, are the foundation for the global competitiveness of U.S. and European services companies.

» The EU ranks number one in each major category of global services trade in 2012, but exports of services from Europe declined by 2.3% due to depressed economic conditions. Services exports plunged 5.7% from France; 3.3% from the UK; and 1.l% from Germany. U.S. services exports, in contrast, rose 5.5% in 2012.

» Five of the top ten export markets for U.S. services are in Europe. Europe accounted for 38.1% of total U.S. services exports and for 41.6% of total U.S. services imports in 2012.

» U.S. services exports to the EU more than doubled between 2001 and 2012, rising from around $102 billion to $240 billion. U.S. services exports to Europe grew 3.8% to total $239 billion in 2012. The U.S. enjoyed a $66.8 billion trade surplus in services with Europe in 2012, compared with its $126 billion trade deficit in goods with Europe. In the first nine months of 2013, U.S. services exports to Europe grew 5.3% to total $187 billion.

» Moreover, foreign affiliate sales of services, or the delivery of transatlantic services by foreign affiliates, have exploded on both sides of the Atlantic over the past few decades and become far more important than exports, topping more than $1 trillion.

» Sales of services by U.S. foreign affiliates in Europe—$645 billion in 2010—were more than two and half times U.S. services exports to Europe in 2011.

» The UK alone accounted for around 30% of all U.S. affiliate sales in Europe in 2011—$191 billion, more than combined U.S. affiliate sales of services in South and Central America ($111 billion), Africa ($13 billion) and the Middle East ($29 billion).

» On a global basis, Europe accounted for half of total U.S. services sales.

» U.S. affiliate sales of services in the EU continue to exceed sales of services by U.S. affiliates of European firms. The latter totaled $467 billion in 2011, the former some $645 billion. However, French and German affiliates sold more services in the U.S. than American affiliates sold in France and Germany. European affiliate sales of services were more than 2.5 times larger than U.S. services imports—a fact that underscores the ever-widening presence of European services leaders in the U.S. economy.

Transatlantic Jobs

» Despite stories about U.S. and European companies decamping for cheap labor markets in Mexico or Asia, most foreigners working for U.S. companies outside the U.S. are Europeans, and most foreigners working for European companies outside the EU are American.

» European companies in the U.S. employ millions of American workers and are the largest source of onshored jobs in America. Similarly, U.S. companies in Europe employ millions of European workers and are the largest source of onshored jobs in Europe.

» U.S. affiliates directly employ about 4.2 million workers in Europe. According to estimates, U.S. affiliates added 106,000 new jobs to the UK economy in 2012, created 58,800 new jobs in Germany, 17,000 new jobs in the Czech Republic, 13,000 new jobs in the Netherlands and 7,000 jobs in Spain. But they also cut about 9,000 jobs in Italy and over 40,000 jobs in France.

» Roughly 35% of the 11.8 million people employed by U.S. majority-owned affiliates around the world in 2012 lived in Europe; roughly half work in the UK, Germany and France.

» U.S. affiliates employed more manufacturing workers in Europe in 2011 (1.8 million) than they did in 1990 (1.6 million), but somewhat less than in 2000 (1.9 million). Moreover, manufacturing employment has declined in some countries while gaining in others.

» The largest declines in manufacturing employment among U.S. affiliates were reported in the UK, with the total manufacturing work force declining to 301,000 in 2011 from 431,000 in 2000. Employment in France dropped from 249,000 to 199,000, and a decline from 388,000 to 359,000 was recorded in Germany, although there was a net gain of U.S. affiliate employment in Germany of 8,000 in 2011 from 2010.

» Poland has been a big winner: U.S. affiliates employ over 100,000 workers in Poland today, twice as many as in 2000, and more than in Spain (86,300), Ireland (52,200), or even Japan (77,000).

» U.S. affiliates in Poland, the Czech Republic, Slovakia and Hungary now employ roughly 230,000 manufacturing workers, more than in France (roughly 200,000), in Italy (96,800), India (148,600), South Korea (57,200), Thailand (103,700) and all of Africa (91,800).

» U.S. affiliates employ more Europeans in services than in manufacturing and on balance are hiring more people in the services sector than in manufacturing. Manufacturing accounted for just 42.5% of total employment by U.S. affiliates in Europe in 2011. U.S. affiliates employed nearly 373,000 workers in transportation and 264,000 in chemicals. Wholesale employment was among the largest sources of services-related employment, which includes employment in such areas as logistics, trade, insurance and other related activities.

» The manufacturing workforce of U.S. affiliates in Germany totaled 360,000 workers in 2011—above the number of manufactured workers employed in Brazil by U.S. affiliates (316,000) and India (149,000) yet below the figures of China (574,000).

» European majority-owned foreign affiliates directly employed roughly 3.8 million U.S. workers in 2012—some 500,000 less workers than U.S. affiliates employed in Europe. The top five European employers in the U.S. in 2012 were firms from the UK (986,000, up from 910,000 in 2011), Germany (600,000, up from 589,000 in 2011), France (531,000, up from 489,000 in 2011), Switzerland (457,000, up from 416,000 in 2011) and the Netherlands (405,000, up from 350,000 in 2011). European firms employed two-thirds of all U.S. workers on the payrolls of majority-owned foreign affiliates in 2012.

» The top five U.S. states in terms of jobs provided directly by European affiliates in 2011 were California (298,800), New York (237,900), Texas (226,400), Pennsylvania (167,500) and Illinois (145,500).

The Transatlantic Innovation Economy

» Bilateral U.S.-EU flows in R&D are the most intense between any two international partners. In 2011 U.S. affiliates invested $27.7 billion in research and development in Europe, $3.3 billion more than in 2010, representing roughly 61% of total global R&D expenditures by U.S. foreign affiliates of $45.7 billion.

» R&D expenditures by U.S. affiliates were greatest in Germany, the UK, Switzerland, France, the Netherlands, Belgium and Ireland. These seven countries accounted for 86% of U.S. global spending on R&D in Europe in 2011.

» In the U.S, R&D expenditures by majority-owned foreign affiliates totaled nearly $45.2 billion in 2011. R&D spending by European affiliates totaled $33.4 billion, $2.1 billion more than in 2010, and representing three-fourths of all R&D performed by majority-owned foreign affiliates in the United States.

» Swiss-owned R&D in the U.S. totaled $8.9 billion in 2011, nearly one-fifth of total affiliate R&D in the United States. British, German and French affiliates accounted for 14.2%, 12.2% and 11.1% shares respectively.

CHAPTER 1

HEADLINE TRENDS:
A Pivotal Year for the Transatlantic Economic Partnership

More than five years after the U.S.-led global financial crisis and recession, the global economy is still struggling to find its footing. Global growth of 3.0% in 2013 was again below the long-term average of 3.7%, marking three consecutive years of subpar growth for the world. In 2013, the U.S. economy expanded by 1.9%, while growth in the euro area contracted 0.4%, following a 0.7% decline in 2012. Growth in Japan was better—1.7% in 2013. For the developed countries as a whole, the economic expansion was rather feeble last year—clocking in at just 1.3%.

Even the developing countries struggled in 2013, achieving growth of just 4.7%, the second consecutive year of sub-5% growth for this cohort. Remove China from the mix, and emerging market growth was even weaker than the headline figure. Over the course of the year, Brazil, Russia, India and many other emerging markets failed to maintain forward economic momentum. The U.S. economy grew just as fast, if not faster, than Brazil, South Africa and many other emerging markets. China underperformed as well, with real GDP growth of 7.7% in 2013—that's good but not great by China's standards, and well off the 10% growth levels of just a few years ago.

Here's 2013's silver lining: global economic activity, led by the U.S., picked up in the second half of the year, with the U.S. economy expanding by an annualized rate of 4.1% in the third quarter and 3.2% in the fourth quarter. Pleasantly surprising to virtually everyone, the U.S. unemployment rate dropped to 6.7% by December 2013 and ticked lower (6.6%) in January 2014. Thanks to a robust stock market and a rebound in home prices, the net worth of U.S. households continued to rise over 2013, boosting consumer confidence and spending over the balance of the year. Corporate earnings ended the year at near-record highs, while America's energy revolution helped to boost U.S. trade figures and U.S. global competitiveness.

Notwithstanding all of the above, the key question for the U.S. economy is the following: can the economy reach and sustain growth in the 3.0-3.5% range without the extraordinary help of the U.S. Federal Reserve, which has pumped unprecedented levels of liquidity into the U.S. economy since the collapse of Lehman Brothers in September 2008? As the Federal Reserve "tapers," or removes liquidity from the credit markets, will the U.S. economy be able to stand on its own two feet?

We believe the U.S. economy will achieve growth in excess of 3% in 2014, with consumption, investment and trade leading the way. There will be less of a fiscal drag in 2014, adding more forward economic momentum. For some perspective on the fiscal drag in 2013, the squeeze on fiscal spending was 2.7% of GDP, according to the OECD, which equates to one of the biggest belt-tightening packages since World War II.

Meanwhile, the balance sheets of U.S. households and U.S. corporations are robust, which should support rising consumption and investment levels this year. Even the finances of the U.S. federal government have improved (at least in the short run), with the U.S. federal budget deficit (in an absolute and relative sense) improving sharply in 2013. Add to the above: manufacturing activity has revived; productivity rates continue to improve; inflationary pressures remain mute; wages are tame; the U.S. housing and automobile markets remain robust; and foreign capital inflows to the U.S. remain strong, providing the U.S. economy with liquidity even in the face of Fed "tapering."

2014 is a pivotal year for the United States. It should be the year the economy finally escapes from the devastating and lingering effects of the financial crisis of 2008.

It's also a pivotal year for Europe. Across the pond, the question is whether or not the European Union can advance and build on the fragile economic recovery of

TABLE 1: U.S. VS. EURO AREA - REAL GDP, ANNUAL PERCENT CHANGE

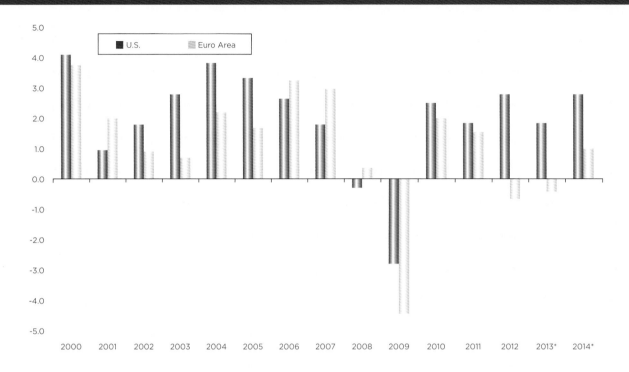

* 2013: Estimate; 2014: Forecast.
Source: IMF

2013. The acute phase of the euro crisis is over—that is the good news. The not-so-encouraging news is that Europe's economic recovery remains very shaky—deflation, stagnant economic activity, and stubbornly high unemployment levels all remain real threats to Europe's rebound. The region's recession technically ended in the first quarter of 2013. However, subsequent growth has been anemic and driven in large part by increased activity from Germany, Europe's strongest and largest economy. Presently, while Ireland, Portugal and Spain are in recovery mode—with much of Europe's periphery now running current account surpluses—France and Italy have slipped back into recession, placing a sizable drag on growth for the continent. How much traction can Europe gain if France doesn't grow, considering that the French economy is the second largest in Europe after Germany? Italy is the fourth largest economy, and the country's continuing woes represent another potential drag on overall EU growth.

What's more, the deleveraging that has transpired in the United States has yet to really happen in Europe. Private sector debt remains a key concern in Europe, with total domestic non-financial sector debt (households, non-financial firms, and the general government) some 232% of GDP at the end of 2012, up from 203% of GDP in 2007. In addition, European banks are not as well capitalized

as their U.S. counterparts; hence in 2014, the European Central Bank (ECB) will assess the banks' balance sheets as part of its Asset Quality Review, with some banks expected to fail, placing more strain on European credit markets. The sector will come out stronger in the end from the exercise, but near-term credit volatility is expected.

Given all of the above, the pivotal question for Europe is this: can the region build on the fragile foundation upon which it sits? Can policy makers in Brussels, at the ECB, and in national capitals work together to turn the recovery into a full-fledged expansion, or will Europe backslide into recession, creating more problems for itself and its transatlantic partner, the United States?

Our hunch is that Europe will muddle through this year, not backslide on growth, and slowly rebuild a competitive base for future growth. But many risks remain.

Finally, 2014 is also a pivotal year for the U.S. and Europe together, as the two partners negotiate a potentially transformative Transatlantic Trade and Investment Partnership (TTIP).

Over the past year, while the negotiators from the U.S. and Europe negotiated, reams of analysis and commentary were

TABLE 2: CURRENT ACCOUNT BALANCE OF PIIGS (1-YEAR MOVING TOTAL, BILLIONS OF $)

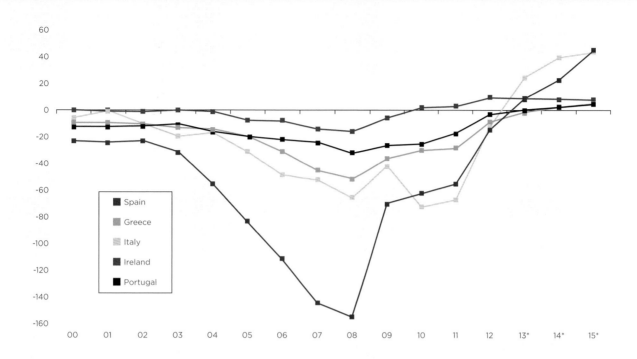

*Projections by the Organization for Economic Co-operation and Development (OECD)
Source: OECD.*

manufactured on both sides of the pond, with the general consensus being that the benefits of TTIP would outweigh the costs and that the deal should get done. Whether this happens remains to be seen, however; TTIP faces formidable political pressures and obstacles on both sides of the pond. It is unlikely that a deal would be concluded this year.

That said, why TTIP?

The Benefits from a Comprehensive TTIP Agreement

At first glance, the idea that the United States should hitch its wagon to struggling Europe via comprehensive arrangements on free trade, investment and other areas could appear misguided. Yet such a comprehensive agreement would grant U.S. companies greater market access to the world's largest and wealthiest economy— the European Union (EU)—and help drive future sales and earnings for many firms. Conversely, for numerous European firms already embedded in the United States, a transatlantic pact would help strip away multiple barriers to doing business in the U.S., boosting sales and profits over the long-term as well.

The deal, in short, would be a win-win for both sides, and not just for U.S. and European multinationals. Small and medium-sized firms could in fact be the main beneficiaries. While a high degree of market integration already exists between the U.S. and Europe thanks to past and existing trade and investment agreements, much more can be done to fuse the world's two largest economies together. A transatlantic agreement would reduce tariffs to near zero across most product categories, but even greater gains would be realized through reductions in non-tariff barriers and harmonizing the web of regulatory standards that inhibits transatlantic trade and investment flows and adds to the cost of doing business on both sides of the ocean.

We are not talking about sexy topics here: recognizing each other's food safety standards to be compatible or essentially equivalent; establishing e-commerce protocols; resolving data privacy issues; standardizing a myriad of services-related activities in such sectors as aviation, retail trade, maritime, telecommunications, procurement rules and regulations; and promoting "upstream" regulatory cooperation for new technologies. The move towards a more barrier-free transatlantic market would also include product standardization so that a car tested for safety in Stuttgart can be sold without further tests in Spartanburg. Or a drug approved by the Federal Drug Administration in Washington is deemed safe and market-ready in Brussels.

Technical regulations and safety standards are not exciting topics. But when these hurdles to doing business are stripped away, the end results are lower costs for companies and greater demand for their goods and services. Consider the crash test dummy. U.S. carmakers run their autos into walls with essentially the same human-dimensioned test device aboard as do European carmakers. Safety standards are high and similar. Yet to export their cars, automakers must run the test again to meet the other government's measurement standards. If the United States and the European Union would recognize each other's crash tests and related standards, estimates are that price savings could range up to 7% on each car or truck.[1] Another example is packaging of pharmaceutical products in both the U.S. and Europe. Reuters cites a German pharmaceutical executive as saying that when selling asthma inhalers in both the U.S. and Europe, the company had to spend $10 million just to prepare the product for the two markets because of the two different standards of dose counters.

Given the influence of the transatlantic economy, U.S.-EU standards are likely to set the tone for global standards, reducing the likelihood that other nations like China would impose protectionist or less safe or healthy requirements for products or services.

An agreement that included efforts to remove barriers to services would have an even greater impact on jobs and growth. As we have documented elsewhere,[2] services represent the sleeping giant of the transatlantic economy. Most American and European jobs are in the services economy, which accounts for over 70% of U.S. and EU GDP. The U.S. and EU are each other's most important commercial partners and major growth markets when it comes to services trade and investment. Deep transatlantic connections in services industries, provided by mutual investment flows, are not only important in their own right; they are also the foundation for the global competitiveness of U.S. and European services companies. A good share of U.S. services exports to the world are generated by European companies based in the U.S., just as a good share of EU services exports to the world are generated by U.S. companies based in Europe. Yet protected services sectors on both sides of the Atlantic account for about 20% of combined U.S.-EU GDP—more than the protected agricultural and manufacturing sectors combined. Major services sectors such as electricity, transport, distribution and business services suffer from particularly high levels of protection. A targeted opening of services could present vast opportunities to firms and huge gains to consumers in both the EU and the United States. Removing barriers in these sectors would be equivalent to 50 years' worth of

GATT and WTO liberalization of trade in goods. An initial transatlantic initiative could be a building block for more global arrangements. Such negotiations would be likely to trigger plurilateral negotiations to include other partners.

As for tariffs, average transatlantic tariffs are relatively low, at about 3-4% on average, although tariffs remain quite high in such categories as agriculture, textiles and apparel, and footwear. So there is room for barriers to come down. In addition, since the volume of U.S.-EU trade is so huge, eliminating even relatively low tariffs could boost trade significantly. A report by the European think tank ECIPE estimated that a transatlantic zero-tariff agreement could boost U.S. and EU exports each by 17%—about five times more than under the recent U.S.-Korea free trade agreement.[3] Moreover, since a large percentage of transatlantic trade is intra-firm, or trade in parts and components within the firm, even small tariffs can add to the cost of production and result in higher prices for consumers on both sides of the ocean. The more intense the intra-industry trade component of trade between two parties, like the one that characterizes U.S.-EU commerce, the greater the effects and benefits of lower tariffs.

At a broader and more macro level, a study by the EU Commission found that eliminating or harmonizing half of all non-tariff barriers on bilateral commerce would add 0.7% to the size of the EU's economy and 0.3% to America's economy by 2018. Such an effort would be 3 times more beneficial to the U.S. and EU economies than current offers on the negotiating table in the Doha Round regarding manufacturing, services and sectoral agreements.[4] Even a 25% reduction in non-tariff barriers could lead to a $106 billion increase in combined EU and U.S. GDP.

Such a deal would help create jobs and income on both sides of the Atlantic, and give U.S. and European firms a leg up in the world's two largest markets, the European Union and the United States.

The bottom line is this: while a U.S.-EU "free trade plus" deal may sound illogical right now for numerous reasons, such a deal makes plenty of sense for both parties over the long term. Trade pacts may not be exciting and rarely garner the attention of Wall Street. But this deal would be a blockbuster and help revive and reinvigorate the transatlantic economy and U.S. and European firms embedded on both sides of the pond. The geo-strategic implications of such a deal would also be significant. If leaders on both sides of the Atlantic grasp the moment, the first U.S. 'Pacific President' and his EU partners may well become best known for having re-founded the Atlantic Partnership.

TABLE 3: THE FOUR ENGINES OF THE WORLD ECONOMY (% OF WORLD TOTAL, 2012)

	Engine One: North America	Engine Two: Europe	Engine Three: Asia	Engine Four: Commodity Producers
GDP (Purchasing Power Parity)	21.3	20.8	36.5	21.4
Population	5.0	8.6	55.8	30.6
Private Consumption Expenditure*	29.3	25.3	26.8	18.6
Exports	11.4	34.8	33.0	20.8
Imports	15.7	34.1	32.7	17.5
International Reserves**	2.0	13.2	57.8	27.1

Sources: IMF, UN
*Personal or household consumption expenditure
**Excluding gold

In the end, transatlantic economic activity will pivot on three variables in 2014. First, the level of activity (think trade, investment, profits, employment, etc.) will be determined by whether or not the U.S. economy finally breaks free from the lingering effects of the 2008-09 recession and expands/grows by better than 3% annually this year. Second, activity will be determined by Europe's ability to avoid an economic relapse or recession this year, and continue to build on the fragile recovery of 2013. Finally, transatlantic commerce will be influenced by the TTIP negotiations—whether or not U.S. and EU trade negotiators can demonstrate tangible progress toward reaching one of the most ambitious and far-reaching commercial agreements in history in the face of stiff political headwinds on both sides of the pond. A successful deal would be a catalyst for more transatlantic trade and investment, and its positive spillover effects. Failure, on the other hand, could be a demoralizer and disincentive to more transatlantic business and commerce.

Time will tell. In the meantime, it is worth underscoring the importance of Europe in the world economy by revisiting our model framework— the world economy as a Boeing 747.

Europe's Place in the Global Economy

When framing Europe's role in the global economy, it is useful to think of the world economy as a four-engine Boeing 747. Engine Number One is composed of the United States and Canada, accounting for over one-fifth of world GDP based on purchasing power parity, according to the IMF. Although Engine One is home to just 5% of the world population, this engine nevertheless accounts for 29.3% of global consumption and for 15.7% of world imports. These are impressive figures. But the numbers are even larger when considering Engine Two.

Engine Two consists of the 28 member states of the European Union and a few neighboring countries like

Switzerland and Norway. This engine accounts for 21% of world GDP and over one-quarter of global consumption. The EU is the world's largest exporting entity and the world's largest trader in goods and services. It is the top supplier of goods to developing countries and is the largest trading partner of each of the BRICs—Brazil, Russia, India, China. It is the largest provider and recipient of foreign direct investment among all world regions. These metrics underscore the fact that Europe plays a key role in keeping the global economy aloft. Against this backdrop, it is little wonder that Europe's lingering sovereign debt crisis and depressed growth levels have placed a tremendous strain on the other engines of the world economy.

Engine Three is Asia, the largest region in the world in terms of output and population. This engine stretches from India to Japan, and as we have learned in the past four years, Engine Three cannot fly solo. Weakness in Engine Two (Europe) has translated into declining exports from Asia, notably China, reducing real economic growth rates across the region.

Europe still matters—just ask thousands of Asian exporters whose orders and revenues have declined on account of the eurozone crisis. Or ask the commodity producers who make up the bulk of Engine Four. Their export receipts have declined sharply over the past few years due to softening global demand. Although this is a diverse group, encompassing such regions as Latin America, the Middle East, Russia, central Asia, central Europe and Africa, the common link holding Engine Four together is their combined role as the world's supplier of primary commodities. Their fortunes are tied to global economic activity—rising global output is typically associated with rising commodity prices, and vice versa. Hence, with Europe acting as a significant drag on global growth, the pain and aftershocks have been felt far and wide among the world's commodity exporters.

TABLE 4: COUNTRIES' BANKS: CROSS-BORDER EXPOSURE (AS OF END SEPTEMBER 2013)

Exposure to...	Belgian banks	French banks	German banks	Greek banks	Irish banks	Italian banks	Portuguese banks	Spanish banks	UK banks	U.S. banks
Belgium		$224.134	$32.4 bn	$292 m	$206 m	$5.1 bn	$172 m	$6.1 bn	$16.4 bn	$19.7 bn
France	$31.2 bn		$204.3 bn	$1.5 bn	$5.5 bn	$40.0 bn	$5.3 bn	$41.1 bn	$224.5 bn	$226.7 bn
Germany	$10.7 bn	$199.4 bn		$2.3 bn	$1.7 bn	$235.8 bn	$1.2 bn	$59.3 bn	$174.6 bn	$162.5 bn
Greece	$5 m	$2.1 bn	$30.6 bn		$190 m	$1.5 bn	$166 m	$632 m	$11.9 bn	$11.4 bn
Ireland	$19.6 bn	$37.9 bn	$70.8 bn	$319 m		$9.8 bn	$6.8 bn	$5.3 bn	$120.3 bn	$62.0 bn
Italy	$10.0 bn	$345.8 bn	$126.8 bn	$562 m	$662 m		$4.2 bn	$27.8 bn	$47.7 bn	$47.9 bn
Portugal	$430 m	$15.7 bn	$22.4 bn	$24 m	$359 m	$1.5 bn		$72.0 bn	$14.6 bn	$3.8 bn
Spain	$12.2 bn	$107.0 bn	$124.1 bn	$215 m	$3.0 bn	$21.0 bn	$20.1 bn		$84.6 bn	$52.1 bn
UK	$24.9 bn	$174.7 bn	$452.1 bn	$10.7 bn	$91.8 bn	$51.9 bn	$3.2 bn	$394.0 bn		$545.1 bn

Exposure to Belgium and Greece as of the end of June 2013.
Sources: Bank for International Settlements; Financial Times.
Data for foreign claims by nationality of reporting banks, immediate borrower basis.

All of the above serves as a template by which to view the world economy. Too much attention is typically paid to the United States and Asia, led by China, as key growth engines of the world, with only passing consideration given to Europe. Yet Europe's economic weight and stature is just as critical. Europe matters—a fact the world has painfully come to realize over the past few years.

How the Eurozone Crisis has been Transmitted to the United States

The dense weave of U.S.-European commercial interconnections amplifies both positive and negative economic trends across the Atlantic. Just as the U.S. financial crisis had a major impact on the European economy, the European financial crisis has affected U.S. economic prospects. The contagion has been transmitted to the United States via three channels—through the capital markets, through trade and investment, and through U.S. corporate earnings. Each channel is discussed briefly below.

Channel One: The Credit and Capital Markets

One of the most direct ways Europe's financial crisis has manifested itself in the U.S. has been through shifting money flows in the transatlantic capital markets, the largest in the world. Transatlantic capital flows have been quite volatile since the U.S. financial crisis, which dramatically curtailed the cross-border movement of capital as banks and other nonfinancial institutions globally retrenched and redirected capital back home. U.S. banks pulled money out of Europe and European banks pulled capital out of the United States, an expected and rational response in times of financial stress and uncertainty. In addition, with bank capital requirements

soaring on both sides of the Atlantic, U.S. and European banks have had to rebuild their capital base through asset sales, reduced deal financing and less cross-border lending, resulting in a corresponding weakening in cross-border flows.

Europe's sovereign debt crisis only served to make banks even more risk-adverse, although as mentioned above, a more aggressive ECB has helped alleviate credit fears over a possible sovereign default. The credit cycle in Europe is gradually improving. That said, however, Europe remains highly financially interdependent, hence the lingering fear that financial stress in one corner of the eurozone will quickly spread to others.

Table 4 underscores this interdependence. Notice the exposure of German banks to Spain, Greece and Portugal. At the end of September 2013 Germany's bank exposure totaled roughly $31 billion to Greece and $22 billion to Portugal, but a staggering $124 billion in Spain. French banks have significant exposure in Italy ($346 billion) and Spain ($107 billion). These numbers have declined over the past few years but nevertheless remain significant. Given this deep interdependence, it is easy to understand the mounting panic in global capital markets over 2010-12 when Europe's sovereign debt crisis threatened a number of countries. The good news is that the panic has subsided; ECB President Mario Draghi's pledge of "whatever it takes" in the summer 2012, supported by German Chancellor Angela Merkel's determination that the euro would not fail, helped break the cycle of fear and financial panic, and was instrumental in engender confidence across the continent last year.

As for the United States, given the interdependence of the transatlantic capital markets, Wall Street has not been spared Europe's financial crisis. U.S. banks are not overly exposed to either Greece or Portugal: outstanding U.S. loans/claims in Greece totaled just $11 billion and $3.8 billion in Portugal in late 2013. Yet U.S. financial institutions are quite heavily exposed to the United Kingdom, Italy, France and Germany, which in turn are highly leveraged to some of Europe's most financially stressed nations. Transatlantic financial linkages, in other words, are thick and very much entangled across borders, meaning that a financial problem in one nation in the eurozone is a problem for the entire continent, and potentially the United States.

Against this backdrop, portfolio flows from Europe to the United States declined again in 2013, and sharply. According to figures from the U.S. Treasury Department, purchases of U.S. assets (U.S. Treasuries, government agency bonds, corporate bonds, and equities) from the EU15 (or developed Europe) plunged 16% in the first eleven months of 2013 versus the same period a year ago. EU15 purchases of U.S. Treasuries declined by 58% over the period, while purchases of U.S. equities were down 33%. In total, portfolio inflows from the EU15 amounted to roughly $115 billion last year, one of the lowest levels since the early 1990s.

This plunge reflects the credit and capital stress of Europe, with more investors—private and public—needing to raise capital at home to cover their expenses and credit obligations. The downturn also reflects, in part, investor unease with how the U.S. government conducts business, with the government shutdown in late 2013 leading to large selling of U.S. securities among foreigners.

As for foreign direct investment flows, FDI inflows from Europe to the United States have also trailed off over the past few years. Indeed, in the first nine months of 2013, European FDI to the U.S. plunged 37% from the same period a year earlier. This came on the heels of a 17.7% decline in inflows in 2012. For the year, we estimate that Europe's FDI investment in the United States totaled roughly $80 billion, one of the weakest levels in years.

But last year's decline is attributable to massive disinvestment (or outflows) from Belgium, a point worth highlighting. U.S. FDI inflows from Belgium in the first three quarters of 2013 were a net -$13.3 billion, a massive disinvestment figure that distorts total FDI inflows. Indeed, excluding Belgium, FDI inflows from Europe to the U.S. dropped by 7.6% as opposed to the 37% decline with Belgium included in the figures.

By country, FDI inflows from Germany to the United States plunged 118% from the same period a year earlier; year-over-year declines were also posted by the Netherlands (-30%), France (-66%), Sweden (-108%), and the United Kingdom (-10%). In general, recessionary conditions in Europe have hampered the global expansion plans of many European firms, many of which facing declining earnings at home, higher capital costs and greater caution on the part of senior management. All of these factors have converged to lower European FDI flows to the United States.

Channel Two: Cross-Border Trade and Investment

Not unexpectedly, America's trade deficit with the European Union widened again in 2013, with the U.S. posting a $125 billion merchandise trade deficit with the EU for the year. The figure was 8% larger than the prior year but more than double the deficit in 2009 ($60 billion).

Germany, incidentally, accounted for just over half the deficit, with the U.S. posting a $67 billion trade deficit with Europe's largest economy in 2013, a rise of 12.2% from the levels of 2012. In 2013, U.S. exports to Germany fell 2.8%, to $47.4 billion, while imports rose 5.5%, to $114.6 billion.

U.S. exports posted gains to Belgium (+7.7%), France (3.8%), Italy (2.6%), the Netherlands (5%) and a host of smaller nations in 2013. The largest declines were reported with Ireland (-10.4%), Sweden (-17.9%) and the United Kingdom (-13.7%). After Germany, the U.S. posted large trade deficits with France ($13.3 billion), Ireland ($25 billion), Italy ($22.1 billion), and the United Kingdom ($5.3 billion).

In this context it is important to note that while the United States has been registering consistent merchandise trade deficits with Europe, it also continues to register consistent services trade surpluses with Europe. While the services data is not up to date as the merchandise trade data, the trends are clear. In 2012 the United States enjoyed a near $67 billion trade surplus in services with all of Europe, and in the first nine months of 2013 the United States posted a $51 billion trade surplus in services with Europe.

Channel Three: U.S. Corporate Earnings

Finally, it is not just finance and trade where the ill effects of the European crisis have hurt the United States. The impact has also been evident in earnings—the bottom line—of many U.S. corporations. Whether autos and capital goods, or high-end retail or transportation, numerous American firms have struggled to post profits in Europe since the financial crisis started in late 2010.

TABLE 5: CORPORATE AMERICA'S BIAS TOWARD EUROPE
(U.S. FOREIGN DIRECT INVESTMENT (FDI) OUTFLOWS TO EUROPE AS A PERCENT OF TOTAL)

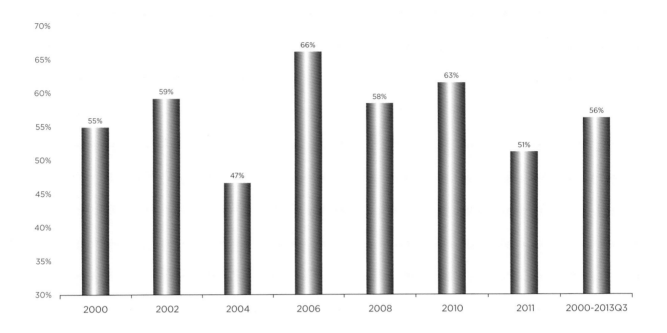

Source: Bureau of Economic Analysis
Data through 3Q2013

When Europe struggles, so does a large part of Corporate America, given the region's outsized influence on corporate profits. No other region of the world is as important to the global success of U.S. multinationals as Europe, due to the simple fact that over the past few decades no place in the world has attracted more U.S. foreign direct investment than Europe. Over the 1980s, for instance, Europe accounted for 55% of total cumulative outflows from the United States. Europe's aggregate share of U.S. investment dipped to 53.5% in the 1990s before rebounding in the first decade of this century, edging up to 55% of the global total.

Not much has changed in this decade thus far. Although Europe has been in the throes of a financial crisis, since the start of this century it has attracted just over 56% of total U.S. investment (see Table 5). That is a robust share considering the emergence of rising markets elsewhere and all the misplaced hype about U.S. firms decamping from high-cost locales—the U.S. and Europe—for cheaper destinations in China and India. The evidence suggests otherwise.

Table 6 offers numerous metrics—the number of foreign affiliates, affiliate employment, R&D expenditures, compensation, total assets—that rank Europe at the top of the list. In good times, these transmission belts of economic integration amplify opportunities for growth, profits and jobs. But by the same token, when things go sour, as they have in the past few years in Europe, the ill effects are quickly transmitted to the bottom line of many U.S. multinationals.

These interlinkages meant that U.S. affiliates registered a slight gain in income in 2013. U.S. affiliate income—a proxy for the earnings of U.S. companies in Europe—totaled $172 billion in the first nine months of 2013, up slightly, or 1.2% from the same period a year earlier; we estimate that for the year, affiliate income totaled $230 billion. As is typically the case, affiliate income varied by country—declines in income were reported in the first nine months of the year in France (-12%) and Germany (-63%), as well as the recession-weary nations of Greece (-114%) and Italy (-65%). Offsetting increases were reported in Ireland (1.1%), the Netherlands (7%), and the United Kingdom (12.8%).

Near-Term Outlook: The Worse is Over, but Risks Linger

Plenty of risks linger over the transatlantic economy in 2014, but for the most part, the balance is tilted towards more upside surprises than downside disappointments over the near term. As *The Economist* has noted, "the West is looking sprightlier, with output growing simultaneously in its three big regions—America, Japan and Europe—a rarity in recent years."[5]

TABLE 6: EUROPE IS NUMBER ONE FOR U.S. FOREIGN AFFILIATES*

	Value	% of Total	Global Rank**
Number of Affiliates	13,415.0	52.3%	1
Thousands of Employees	4,191.4	35.6%	1
Manufacturing Employment (Thousands)	1,780.9	37.4%	1
Total Assets (Bil. US$)	12,175.1	58.8%	1
Net Property Plant & Equipment (Bil. US$)	450.8	37.5%	1
Total Sales (Bil. US$)	2,847.8	47.7%	1
Sales of Goods	2,052.1	47.1%	1
Sales of Services	698.5	50.3%	1
Net Income (Bil. US$)	621.9	55.8%	1
Capital Expenditures (Bil. US$)	63.6	33.5%	1
R&D Expenditures (Bil. US$)	27.7	60.4%	1
Gross Product ("Value Added", Bil. US$)	697.8	48.3%	1
Compensation of Employees (Bil. US$)	283.3	52.9%	1
The following data is for 2012			
US Foreign Direct Investment Outflows (Bil. US$)	188.5	51.4%	1
Affiliate Income (Bil. US$)	226.4	50.4%	1
Direct Investment Position on a Historical-Cost Basis (Bil. US$)	2,477.0	55.6%	1

Majority-owned bank and nonbank foreign affiliates; data for 2011, latest available.
**Ranked against Canada, Latin America ex. Other Western Hemisphere, Africa, Middle East and Asia & Pacific.*
Source: Bureau of Economic Analysis.

A rarity, indeed. 2014 could turn out to be the year the transatlantic economy becomes more in sync, with 3% plus growth in the United States giving Europe the added lift to reach a stable growth path. Improving prospects in the latter, in turn, would greatly benefit Corporate America's massive investment stakes in Europe. Consumer and business confidence is building on both sides of the pond—a positive setting for the transatlantic economy. However, confidence can be a very fleeting and fickle commodity—here today, gone tomorrow—leaving many constituencies disappointed and frustrated.

Speaking of disappointed and frustrated, any enthusiasm over the near-term outlook for the transatlantic economy has to be tempered by the employment challenges confronting both the United States and Europe. While America's jobless rate has declined to 6.6% of the workforce, the headline figures don't tell the entire story. Structural unemployment remains quite high in the U.S.; the labor force participation rate is declining, while the number of workers considered to be long-term unemployed remains at record levels. Much work remains to be done.

An even greater employment challenge confronts Europe. Employment growth across the continent has been very anemic, with Europe's unemployment rates early in 2014 still stubbornly high and politically dangerous; the swollen ranks of Europe's unemployed remain a lightning rod for social instability. The EU's unemployment rate was 10.8% in November 2013, near a record high, and well beyond the U.S. figures. But more worrisome than the headline figure is the fact that the unemployment rate was higher than 27% in Greece in November 2013 and above 26% in Spain.

Meanwhile, the jobless rate among Europe's youth remains staggering—in November 2013, youth employment (ages 15-24) averaged 23.6% in the EU. In Italy, the figure was 41.6%, 36.8% in Portugal, 57.7% in Spain, and 54.8% in Greece. These figures sometimes include students and other categories of young people that obscure the true state of unemployment, but regardless of specifics, the situation is troubling.

Between the United States and EU, there were some 37.4 million workers counted as unemployed in November 2013, a staggering figure and an astounding waste of human potential.

The swollen ranks of the unemployed on both sides of the pond have fueled a fierce and emotional debate over

Who is America's Dance Partner, Europe or Asia?

There is nothing more fashionable today than writing about Europe's demise, notably in light of Europe's sovereign debt crisis and lingering fears that the euro zone still might break apart. Weak real economic growth, along with threats of deflation and high unemployment, only detract from Europe's allure.

Add it all up and it is easy for American firms to think they should just cut and run from Europe and invest elsewhere. It may be tempting to think that Washington should not waste any political capital on Europe and focus instead on dynamic Asia and the completion of the Trans-Pacific Partnership (TPP) trade pact, an idea that has also gained some traction in the past year. This has become the general consensus. But it is misguided.

As Table 7 highlights, if the U.S. is going to invest energy negotiating a trade agreement with either Europe or Asia, by virtually all metrics a transatlantic deal is where there is more bang for the proverbial buck. The Trans-Pacific Partnership (TPP) does not include either China or India, two of Asia's largest economies. Hence its economic heft is not as sizable as most believe, and underwhelming relative to Europe.

When negotiating with the European Union, the United States is engaging the largest and wealthiest economic entity in the world. Europe's economy is almost 50% larger than the TPP cohort, more populated and far wealthier. The latter is key—the per capita income of the European Union ($32,797) is 33% larger than the nations of TPP.

Not surprisingly, personal consumption in Europe is well above the level of TPP members—$9.7 billion versus $7.1 billion, a 38% difference between TTIP and TPP. Europe is also a much larger exporter and importer than the TPP construct. And finally, as various metrics like FDI, affiliate income, and affiliate sales indicate, Corporate America's greatest stakes are in Europe, not Asia. The Transatlantic Trade and Investment Partnership that the U.S. and EU are now negotiating could deepen these ties to the mutual benefit of both parties.

TABLE 7: COMPARING FREE TRADE AGREEMENTS (BILLIONS OF $ UNLESS OTHERWISE SPECIFIED)

	Transatlantic Trade and Investment Partnership	Trans-Pacific Partnership	NAFTA
GDP (Purchasing Power Parity)	15,993	10,755	3,272
% of World Total	19.2%	12.9%	3.9%
Population (thousands)	508,381	483,649	155,685
% of World Total	7.2%	6.8%	2.2%
Per Capita Income ($)	32,797	24,587	19,262
Personal Consumption Expenditures	9,720	7,066	1,815
% of World Total	23.2%	16.9%	4.3%
Exports	5,583	2,801	824
% of World Total	31.3%	15.7%	4.6%
Imports	5,734	2,934	917
% of World Total	31.1%	15.9%	5.0%
U.S. Outward FDI Stock to...	2,238	934	452
% of U.S. Total	50.3%	21.0%	10.2%
U.S. Inward FDI Stock from...	1,642	620	240
% of U.S. Total	61.9%	23.4%	9.1%
U.S. FDI Income Earned Abroad	196	96	44
% of U.S. Total	43.6%	21.4%	9.8%
Foreign FDI Income Earning in the U.S.	107	37	16
% of U.S. Total	70.9%	24.6%	10.3%
Foreign Affiliate Sales of U.S. MNC's in...*	2,375	1,852	871
% of U.S. Total	39.8%	31.0%	14.6%
U.S. Affiliate Sales of Foreign MNC's from...*	1,857	909	267
% of U.S. Total	52.9%	25.9%	7.6%

Sources: IMF; UN; BEA.
Data for 2012
*Data for 2011

Trading with China: Who Has the Advantage?

U.S. and European multinationals, well entrenched in each other's markets, are scrambling to win the hearts and wallets of Chinese consumers, and for good reason: China is home to one of the largest and fastest growing consumer markets in the world. China now accounts for nearly 10% of world imports, a share greater than any country in Europe. Germany ranked third behind China in 2012; the United States was Number One.

European firms are prime beneficiaries of this little-known fact. They are way out in front of their U.S. counterparts when it comes to providing goods to the Middle Kingdom. For instance, in 2012, EU exports to China totaled $153 billion, some 39% larger than U.S. exports to China. The EU was even ahead of Japan, whose exports to China totaled $144 billion. Germany is the largest exporter to China among European exporters, with Germany exports totaling $68 billion in 2012, the last year of full data. In the first nine months of 2013, EU exports to China amounted to $121 billion, a rise of 6.5% from the same period a year earlier; Japan's exports totaled $94 billion, down 15%, while exports from the U.S. were valued at $83 billion, up 5%. High-end French and Italian luxury items, German automobiles and capital goods, Swiss pharmaceuticals—all of these products have become more attractive to China and help underwrite trade gains with one of the largest and dynamic markets in the world. To this point, German exports to China increased nearly 8-fold 2000 ($8.6 billion) and 2012 ($68 billion). Italy's exports also soared, rising from $2.2 billion at the start of the century to $11.4 billion in 2012. The UK's exports rose from $2.2 billion to $9.5 billion over the same time frame.

The downside is that the U.S., EU and Japan each runs a trade deficit with China, and the trade gap of the U.S. and Europe is quite large.[6] As Tables 8 and 9 highlight, the EU's trade deficit with China totaled $215 billion in 2012, a significant jump from the shortfall in 2000 ($40 billion). The U.S. trade deficit with China was in excess of $333 billion in 2012, and continued to widen in 2013. Japan's imbalance is not as great—less than $40 billion through the first nine months of 2013.

TABLE 8: U.S., EUROPE AND JAPAN EXPORTS TO CHINA - (BILLIONS OF $)

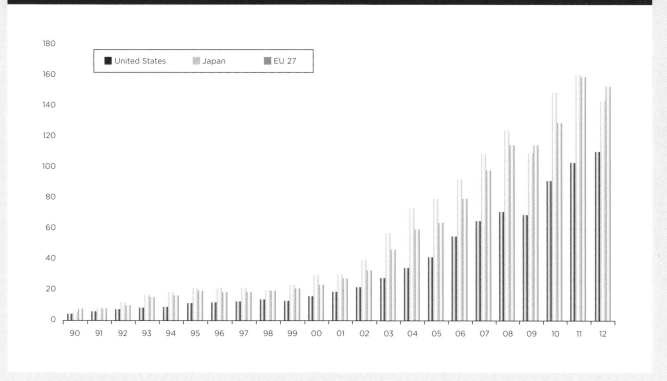

Sources: IMF
Data through 2012

TABLE 9: U.S., EU AND JAPAN TRADE BALANCE WITH CHINA - (BILLIONS OF $)

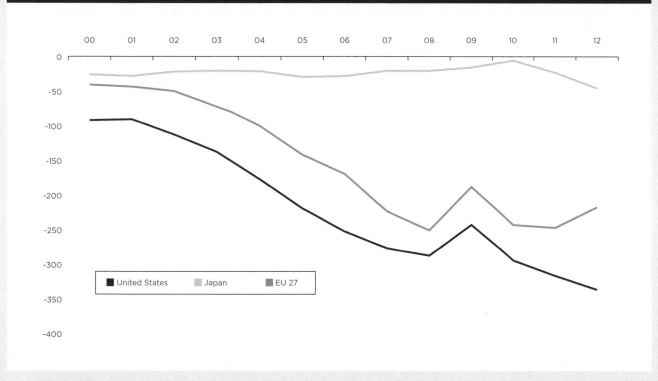

Sources: IMF
Data through 2012

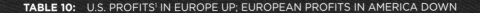

TABLE 10: U.S. PROFITS[1] IN EUROPE UP; EUROPEAN PROFITS IN AMERICA DOWN

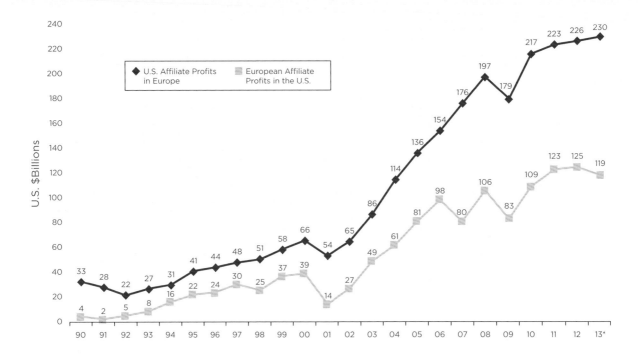

[1]Income of affiliates
*Data through 3Q2013. 2013 data is annualized for full year estimate
Source: Bureau of Economic Analysis

income inequality. Evidence of a widening gulf between "haves" or "have nots" threatens to engender more populist and xenophobic policies across both the United States and Europe. Selling TTIP is not going to be easy against a backdrop of stubbornly high unemployment levels in both the United States and Europe.

The Way Ahead

If there is a silver lining to the transatlantic economy's grim employment picture, it is this: unemployment levels across Europe have peaked, and they are declining in the United States. The figures are still very challenging, but "less bad." Getting the army of idle workers on both sides of the pond back to work is among the key challenges for policy makers.

Another bright spot: as in previous crises over the past decades, the turbulent times of the past few years are set to fade. On both sides of the ocean, real growth is set to resume. Companies are set to hire again. Consumers are becoming less cautious and spending again. Economies are restructuring and resetting. New winners and losers are emerging, like previous crises. To this point, the crisis-stricken nations of the past—like Sweden (1994) and South Korea (1997)—are among the strongest in the

world today. It was not that long ago that Germany was considered the "sick man of Europe;" now Germany ranks as among the strongest in Europe and the world, after it undertook painful reform measures. In other words, today's negative headlines regarding the European debt crisis and America's inability to deal with its structural challenges hardly portend or divine the future.

Who would have guessed that as 2014 began, the developing countries would be the weak link of the global economy? This year will be the first time in three years that both the U.S. and EU economies will be expanding. Growth will be slow and uneven, but the transatlantic pie is poised to expand.

Against this backdrop, key metrics like U.S. capital flows to and from Europe, as well as affiliate income, are likely to remain quite volatile in the near term, and continue to ebb and flow with the transatlantic business cycle. In the first nine months of 2013, U.S. foreign direct investment (FDI) to Europe fell 6.7% from the same period a year earlier. FDI flows to Germany fell sharply after sliding in 2012. Meanwhile, after rebounding in 2012, U.S. investment to France dropped 30% in the first three quarters of 2013 from the same period a year earlier. U.S.

TABLE 11: THE POWER BROKERS OF THE GLOBAL ECONOMY COMPARED

	Eurmerica	Asia	Chindia	Chinmerica
GDP, PPP	39.6%	35.7%	20.4%	34.3%
GDP, Nominal	47.2%	30.7%	13.9%	33.9%
Market cap. (as of 2/11/2014)	$35.9 trillion	$17.8 trillion	$4.6 trillion	$25.2 trillion
Personal consumption exp.	49.9%	29.3%	9.7%	33.8%
M+A Sales	65.8%	17.7%	4.0%	24.7%
M+A Purchases	31.0%	35.9%	12.9%	38.0%
Inward FDI stock	55.4%	24.9%	4.6%	20.9%
Outward FDI stock	69.5%	19.7%	2.7%	24.2%
Inflows (2000-2012)	53.1%	24.9%	8.0%	21.0%
Outflows (2000-2012)	68.8%	19.2%	3.3%	21.3%
Exports* (Goods)	24.7%	42.0%	17.1%	26.2%
Imports* (Goods)	30.2%	40.8%	16.0%	28.8%
Military Spending	$987.2	$385.8	$205.9	$826.4
(U.S. $ billions at constant 2012 prices)	57.0%	22.3%	11.9%	47.7%

Total does not inclu. Intra-EU28 + Norway, Switzerland, & Iceland trade.
Sources: IMF; Bloomberg; UN; SIPRI.
All data for 2011 otherwise noted

outflows to Poland, Ireland and the Netherlands were strong, but outflows were notably weak to the United Kingdom, Spain and a host of other countries.

Overall, U.S. FDI outflows to Europe rose by 6% in 2013, totaling an estimated $200 billion. Not bad for a region deep in crisis and on the verge, allegedly, of a "lost decade."

U.S. FDI inflows from Europe dropped at a steep rate in 2013, or by roughly 24%, to $80 billion. This follows investment inflows of $105 billion in 2012 and $128 billion in 2011, data points that underscore the jaggedness of transatlantic investment flows of late. To a large degree, the downturn in FDI from Europe was less about difficult economic conditions in the United States, and more about European firms (financials) sending capital back home or downsizing their global operations in the face of weakening global demand.

U.S. affiliates in Europe increased their earnings in 2013, although the gains were marginal, with affiliate income rising to $230 billion from $226 billion in 2012. That is a weak performance but still a record high. In the first nine months of the year, affiliate income was relatively flat, with weak affiliate income most notable in France and Germany, where it declined 12% and 63%, respectively, versus a year earlier. The Netherlands, Ireland and the United Kingdom were outliers; affiliate

income rose 12.8% in the UK in the first nine months of the year and 1.1% in Ireland. Income rose 7% in the Netherlands, another key source of European income for U.S. multinationals.

In the U.S., European affiliates posted income declines of 5.5% in the first nine months of the year. For the year, we estimate that European affiliates earned $119 billion; that is sizable sum, but down 4.8% from 2012 record levels.

Trends in transatlantic capital flows reflect many of the variables just mentioned. While Europe remains a key provider of capital to the United States, U.S. capital inflows from the European Union (including the global money centers, the United Kingdom and Luxembourg) dropped again in 2013, as highlighted above. Total inflows amounted to around $115 billion, one of the lowest annual figures in decades. In contrast, U.S. capital outflows to the EU15 totaled roughly $185 billion in 2013, a sharp rise from the previous year ($86 billion). A large part of this gain was related to U.S. investors allocating more capital towards European bonds and equities in anticipation of Europe's economic rebound.

In terms of foreign holdings of U.S. Treasuries, China and Japan still rank number one and two, respectively; as of November 2013, China held $1.3 trillion in Treasuries, or 23% of the total; Japan held $1.2 trillion, or 21% of the total. Europe's total holdings, including those of the UK,

Luxembourg and Switzerland, were in excess of $1 trillion, or on par with Japan, or 21% of the total. OPEC's share was around 4%. In short, it's not just the Asian creditors of China and Japan that are important sources of capital to the U.S. So is Europe.

Finally, the services economies of the United States and Europe have never been as intertwined as they are today, notably in such services activities as financial services, telecommunications, utilities, insurance, advertising, computer services, and other related activities. While the latest figures are not as current as others, it is important to note that five of the top ten export markets for U.S. services are in Europe and that the U.S. enjoyed a near $56 billion trade surplus in services with the EU in 2012, compared with its $116 billion trade deficit in goods with the EU. For all of Europe in 2012, the surplus in services was larger—roughly $67 billion. In the first nine months of 2013, U.S. services exports to Europe totaled $187 billion, a 5.3% rise from the same period a year earlier. Over the same period, the U.S. posted a trade surplus in services with Europe to the tune of $51 billion. Moreover, foreign affiliate sales of services, or the delivery of transatlantic services by foreign affiliates, have exploded on both sides of the Atlantic over the past few decades and become the overwhelming mode of delivery, topping more than $1 trillion. The U.S. and EU are each other's most important commercial partners and major growth markets when it comes to services trade and investment. Moreover, deep transatlantic connections in services industries, provided by mutual investment flows, are the foundation for the global competitiveness of U.S. and European services companies.

In the end, despite the turbulence of past years and a stronger but fragile economic backdrop again in 2014, the United States and Europe remain each other's most important foreign commercial markets, a fact still not fully appreciated by opinion leaders and policy makers on either side of the transatlantic, much less elsewhere around the world. Put simply, no other commercial artery in the world is as integrated and fused together as the transatlantic economy.

We estimate that the transatlantic economy continues to generate over $5.0 trillion in total commercial sales a year and employs up to 15 million workers in mutually "onshored" jobs on both sides of the Atlantic. These workers enjoy high wages, good incomes and high labor and environmental standards. In addition, we continue to espouse the view that the transatlantic economy remains at the forefront of globalization—meaning that the commercial ties between the U.S. and Europe are deeper and thicker than between any other two continents. Recent economic troubles have only underscored the deep integration of the transatlantic economy and the importance of healthy transatlantic economic ties for millions of U.S. and European workers, consumers, and companies. This is quite evident from this survey.

That said, there's more work to do. The transatlantic relationship needs a catalyst, and current efforts towards completing a comprehensive "free trade plus" transatlantic economic agreement is just the undertaking that could breathe new life and more vigor into the world's most important partnership.

TTIP represents a pivotal moment for the U.S. and Europe. It's a pivotal year in general for the United States and Europe, and the transatlantic partnership. Events this year will have a profound effect on the relationship well into this decade and beyond.

Endnotes
1. See the analysis by Garel Rhys in Daniel Hamilton and Joseph P. Quinlan, *Deep Integration: How Transatlantic Markets are Leading Globalization* (Washington, DC: Center for Transatlantic Relations, 2005).
2. Daniel S. Hamilton and Joseph P. Quinlan, *Sleeping Giant: Awakening the Transatlantic Services Economy* (Washington, DC: Center for Transatlantic Relations, 2008).
3. Fredrik Erixon and Matthias Bauer, "A Transatlantic Zero Agreement: Estimating the Gains from Transatlantic Free Trade in Goods," ECIPE Occasional Paper No. 4/2010 (Brussels: ECIPE, 2010). See also Koen Berden, et. al, *The Impact of Free Trade Agreements in the OECD: The Impact of an EU-US FTA, EU-Japan FTA and EU-Australia/New Zealand FTA* (Rotterdam: Ecorys, 2009).
4. Koen Berden, et. al, *Non- Tariff Measures in EU-US Trade and Investment: An Economic Analysis* (Rotterdam: Ecorys, 2009).
5. *The Economist*, The World in 2012, "The West's Turn."
6. New "added value" trade measurements by the OECD and WTO suggest that the trade deficits may be lower than those derived by conventional assessments of gross trade. But the most recent "value added" data stems from 2009, so we have chosen most recent data available, which is derived from conventional trade measurements.

CHAPTER 2

THE POST-CRISIS TRANSATLANTIC ECONOMY:
The Eight Ties that Still Bind

When it comes to global commerce, Europe remains at the center of the universe for Corporate America. This fact has been lost in all the chatter about America's strategic pivot to Asia and daily prophesying from pundits that the future of the world economy lies with the "Rest," notably China. Meanwhile, while there are many areas of disagreement between Washington and Brussels, transatlantic business ties and linkages continue to expand and deepen on a day-to-day basis.

As for the rise of the "Rest," it's interesting to note that in early 2014, it is the emerging markets that are the laggards—not the leaders—of the global economy. For both cyclical and structural reasons, growth has slowed sharply over the past year in Brazil, India, Turkey, South Africa and even China. Rising unemployment, capital outflows, plunging currencies, dissatisfied populations—all of these dynamics and more are dogging emerging market economies in South America, Asia, Africa and the Middle East.

The simple fact of the matter is this: the developing nations are not yet capable of driving global growth in a sustainable fashion. Rather than extolling the strengths of the BRICs—Brazil, Russia, India and China—Wall Street has taken to worrying about the "Fragile Five," or South Africa, Indonesia, Brazil, India and Turkey.

All of the above underscores why the transatlantic partnership remains so important to the United States and to Europe. Yes, the emerging markets are new sources of supply (labor) and demand (consumers) for transatlantic multinationals. But for the bulk of these firms, the core of their global operations center on the United States and Europe. The foundation of the global economy still rests on the shoulders of the U.S.-European partnership.

That said, it has been a rocky decade for the transatlantic economy, defined here as the highly integrated economic space inhabited by the United States and Europe. In the past ten years the transatlantic partnership has been buffeted by economic recessions, military conflicts in the Middle East, a U.S.-led financial crisis-cum-global recession, and Europe's sovereign debt crisis. The latter has made Europe the weak link of the global economy this decade. But the tide has now turned in Europe, and for the better.

As we outlined in our last survey, while Europe's unfolding recession has been well covered by the media, less attention has been paid to underlying trends that should make Europe stronger rather than weaker in the long term. While the pace of economic reform has been muddled and frustratingly slow in many debt-laden nations, the evidence continues to point to improving fundamentals in Europe's periphery. Ireland, Spain and Portugal have all acted decisively over the past few years, and through deregulation, labor market reform, and pro-business tax incentives have raised the competitiveness of their economies. Even the heavy lifting in Greece is starting to pay off, with the government projecting a slight pick-up in growth this year. The outlook in these nations remains fragile, but four years after the sovereign debt crisis erupted in Europe there are clear signs of improvement and progress.

Of course, not all economies in Europe are created equal. Some are more competitive, in better financial shape, and more prudently managed than others. The upshot is a mixed European economic performance, with low-debt, highly competitive economies of the north outperforming debt-laden, uncompetitive economies of the south over the past few years.

Leading U.S. multinationals understand this and invest their money based on their practical experience with European markets. They will continue to leverage the European Union to their strategic advantage. U.S. companies are not moving their investments *out* of Europe, but they do move their investments around *within* Europe, depending on changing circumstance. For instance, U.S. investment in Poland has increased substantially, bringing considerable jobs and helping to generate additional growth for Poland. U.S. investment in Spain, Italy and Greece, on the other hand, has slowed or even gone into reverse.

European firms act similarly within the United States. Even the most skeptical pundits have been surprised by the resiliency of the U.S. economy over the past year, but economic circumstances in one part of the country can differ from other parts, influencing European investment decisions.

As we suggested in our last report, the downturn in transatlantic foreign direct investment in the post-crisis years has been more cyclical than structural, temporary as opposed to permanent.

American and European firms are building out their in-country presence in the developing nations, and for good reasons. Growth rates are above the global average, most populations are young and want Western goods and services, and the technological skill levels of some nations

are now on par with many developed nations. It makes perfect sense for U.S. and European firms to invest outside the transatlantic economy.

But this dynamic does not signal a retreat on the part of U.S. and European firms from the transatlantic economy. It's more about global rebalancing, with many transatlantic firms rushing to deepen their footprint in the developing nations, replicating the deep ties that are the hallmark of the transatlantic partnership. In fact, U.S. and European companies are using global value chains to integrate the value added other countries can contribute to particular products and services into transatlantic bonds of investment and trade.

What makes the transatlantic economy distinctive in this world of rising powers and emerging markets? As we have highlighted in the past, it is foreign investment— the deepest form of global integration—that binds the transatlantic economy together far more than trade. The latter, the cross-border movement of goods and services, is a shallow form of integration and often associated with the early phases or stages of bilateral commerce. In contrast, a relationship that rests on the foundation of foreign

TABLE 1: THE TRANSATLANTIC ECONOMY VS. THE WORLD - SHARE OF WORLD TOTAL

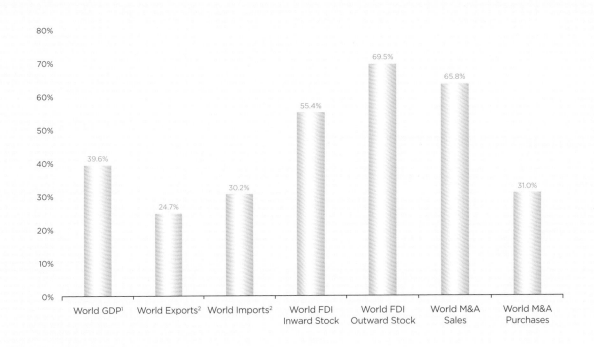

Sources: UN, IMF, figures for 2012.
1. Based on PPP estimates.
2. Excluding intra-EU, Norway, Switzerland and Iceland trade.

investment is one in which both parties are extensively embedded and entrenched in each other's economies. Such a relationship is more job-creating, income-producing, and wealth-generating for both parties than one based solely on trade.

This deep commercial integration epitomizes the transatlantic economy, which is wound and bound together by symbiotic ties between investment and trade in goods and services. Because of this relationship, the global primacy of foreign affiliate sales over trade continues to expand dramatically. To this point, global foreign affiliate sales (sales of affiliates from around the world) in 1990 totaled $5.1 trillion, versus global exports of $4.4 trillion, according to figures from the United Nations. By 2012, however, global foreign affiliate sales tallied a staggering $26 trillion, a figure 16% larger than global exports ($22.4 trillion). The gap between foreign sales and exports reflects in part rising cross-border investment and commerce between the United States and Europe.

Against this backdrop, most American foreign affiliates in Europe are indistinguishable from local German, British, or Dutch firms, while European affiliates operating in the

United States are barely distinguishable to U.S. consumers who enjoy European goods and services on a daily basis without much thought. U.S. firms and their global counterparts in Europe, Japan and now even China, Brazil and other countries prefer to deliver goods and services via foreign direct investment (foreign affiliates) rather than trade (exports).

We do not mean to downplay the importance of transatlantic trade, which remains considerable. Indeed, transatlantic trade (defined here as U.S. exports plus imports of goods from the European Union) totaled an estimated $787 billion in 2013, up from $387 billion at the start of the new century. Transatlantic trade is sizable and important to both economies. But one must add investment to the picture to get a true sense of the size and dynamism of the transatlantic economy, particularly compared to any other bilateral economic relationship either partner has in the world.

Companies invest abroad for various reasons. They may want to make a strategic investment, for instance to introduce a new product or service. "Build where you sell" is a mantra of many successful multinationals, and this requires an

TABLE 2: AMERICA'S MAJOR COMMERCIAL ARTERIES

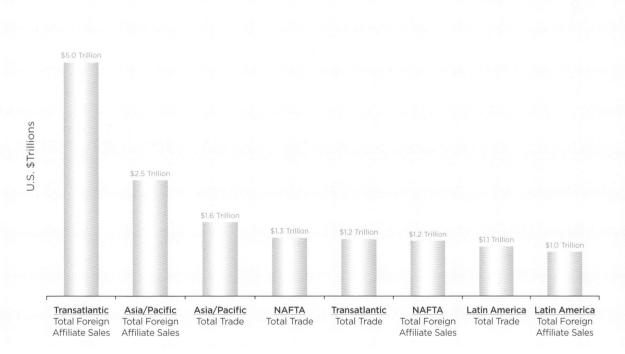

Foreign Affiliate Sales: Estimates for 2012. Total Trade: Data for goods & services, 2012.
Source: Bureau of Economic Analysis.

in-country/region presence in many different parts of the world. They may seek resources, such as acquiring access to specialized knowledge or particular technologies. They may want to win share in new markets, or they may want to achieve greater efficiencies by gaining access to cheap factors of production. While much media and political attention focuses on the resource- or efficiency-seeking motivations behind such investments, particularly the need for cheap foreign labor, the reality is that the increasingly critical need for companies is to position themselves within pan-continental markets, and to generate new sources of knowledge that they can turn into new sources of profit. These latter motivations drive a good deal of mutual investment across the Atlantic.

Moreover, these companies and affiliates invest in local communities. European affiliates in the United States employ millions of American workers and are the largest source of onshored jobs in America. Similarly, U.S. corporate affiliates in Europe employ millions of European workers and are the largest source of onshored jobs in Britain, Ireland and across the European continent.

The Transatlantic Economy in the World

There is no commercial artery in the world as large as the one binding the United States and Europe together. The transatlantic economy still accounts for over 50% of world GDP in terms of value and roughly 40% in terms of purchasing power parity, is the largest and wealthiest market in the world, is at the forefront of global R&D, and drives global foreign direct investment and global mergers and acquisitions activity.

All told, by our estimate roughly $5.0 trillion in commerce takes place between U.S. and European companies and their affiliates each year. Hence, when one half of the transatlantic partnership suffers or goes into recession, like Europe in 2011-12, the other half suffers as well. Europe's problems manifested themselves in declining capital flows from Europe to the U.S., plummeting U.S. exports to Europe, a widening U.S. trade deficit and weaker-than expected U.S. corporate earnings for many companies with extensive links to Europe (think U.S. automakers).

On the flip side, strength in one half of the partnership can have a healing effect on the other. To this point, America's widening trade deficit with Europe—totaling a record $133 billion in 2013—was critical in supporting external growth for Europe against a backdrop of depressed demand at home.

U.S. economic challenges, by the same token, have consequences for Europe, given that the United States is one of the top country export destinations for EU goods and services, the EU's leading source and destination of both FDI and private portfolio investment, and a key innovation partner for European economies seeking to maintain their competitive position in knowledge-based activities. If the United States fails to generate 3%-plus real growth in 2014, the ill effects will be felt not only in the United States but also Europe. Success or failure in one part of the relationship affects the other, since no two regions of the global economy are as economically fused as the two parties straddling the Atlantic.

That said, it has long been our contention that one of the most dangerous deficits affecting the transatlantic partnership is not one of trade, values, or military capabilities but rather a deficit in understanding among opinion leaders of the vital stakes Americans and Europeans have developed in the success of each other's respective economies. Hence, transatlantic differences over financial sector reform and divergences over fiscal and monetary policies, big data and privacy issues, and other critical topics like global climate change are cause for concern. With so much attention devoted to the rise of the Chinese economy and shifting trade flows in both the United States and Europe, many on both sides of the Atlantic have forgotten about the importance of investment and the unappreciated, invisible and little-understood activities of foreign affiliates, which represent the real backbone of the transatlantic economy.

This is illustrated in Table 1, which illustrates the weight of the transatlantic economy in the overall global economy. Taken together, U.S. and European exports to the world accounted for 25% of global exports in 2012; combined U.S. and European imports accounted for 30% of global imports. But the United States and Europe together accounted for 55.4% of the inward stock of foreign direct investment (FDI), and a whopping 69.5% of outward stock of FDI. Moreover, each partner has built up the great majority of that stock in the other economy. In short, mutual investment in the North Atlantic space is very large, dwarfs trade, and has become essential to U.S. and European jobs and prosperity.

All in all, the transatlantic economy remains the dominant force in the global economy. Rising powers are resetting the global economy, but they haven't done so yet. Such a transformation is neither complete nor pre-ordained, as the current crisis in the emerging markets highlights. And a different world economy is not necessarily a worse one for Americans and Europeans—if they use the coming decade to leverage global growth, human talent and innovation while tackling related challenges of deficits and debt, building on their own considerable strengths, and exploiting the full potential of the transatlantic economy. That is a big "if," but each side is laying the groundwork for economic recovery, and both are launching negotiations to further open transatlantic markets and position themselves for the world rising before them.

The Ties that Bind—Quantifying the Transatlantic Economy

It is the activities of foreign affiliates that bind the United States and Europe together. Foreign affiliates on both sides of the Atlantic have constructed a formidable commercial presence in each other's market over the past half century, if not beyond. A handful of U.S. companies sunk roots in Europe over a century ago.

Notwithstanding all the stress and strain on the transatlantic partnership over the past decade, the transatlantic infrastructure remains solid and sturdy. Many measures of economic activity declined sharply in 2009 due to the global recession, rebounded in 2010 and softened again in 2011 and 2012. By the tail end of 2013, many metrics started to improve, reflecting the cyclical rebound in transatlantic economic activity.

Over the past years we have outlined and examined eight key indices that offer a clearer picture of the "deep integration"

forces shaping the transatlantic economy. This chapter updates those indices with the latest available data and our estimates. Each metric, in general, has ebbed and flowed with the cyclical swings of transatlantic economic activity, but has nevertheless grown in size and importance over the past decade.

If there is a common theme to the data below, it is this: most metrics improved over 2013 as the U.S. continued to expand and Europe emerged from recession. More of the same is expected in 2014—thanks to the cyclical upswing in transatlantic economic activity, 2014 is set to be a solid year for affiliates on both sides of the pond.

1. Gross Product of Foreign Affiliates

The best way to think about U.S. and European foreign affiliates is to consider them independent economic entities, since in their own right, U.S. affiliates in Europe and European affiliates in the United States are among the largest and most advanced economic forces in the world. For instance, the total output of U.S. foreign affiliates in Europe (an estimated $760 billion in 2012) and of European foreign affiliates in the U.S. (estimated at $500 billion) was greater than the total gross domestic output of most

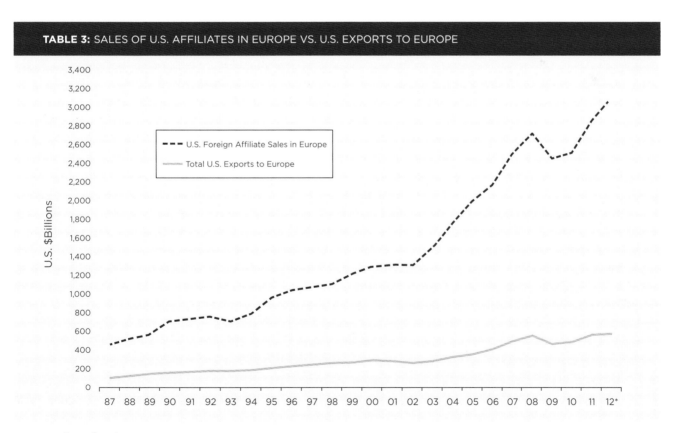

TABLE 3: SALES OF U.S. AFFILIATES IN EUROPE VS. U.S. EXPORTS TO EUROPE

Estimate for sales.
Source: Bureau of Economic Analysis.
Majority-owned non-bank affiliates data: 1987 - 2008. Majority-owned bank and non-bank affiliates: 2009 - 2012.

TABLE 4: SALES OF EUROPEAN AFFILIATES IN THE U.S. VS. U.S. IMPORTS TO EUROPE

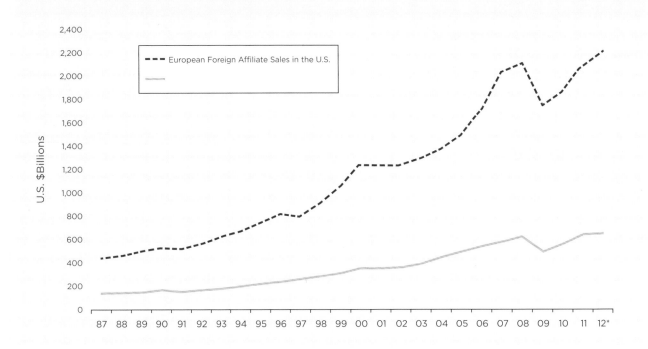

*Estimate for sales
Source: Bureau of Economic Analysis
Majority-owned non-bank affiliates: 1987 - 2006. Majority-owned bank and non-bank affiliates: 2007 - 2012.*

nations. Combined, transatlantic foreign output in 2012—in excess of $1.2 trillion—was larger than the output of such nations as the Netherlands, Turkey or Indonesia.

By our estimation, U.S. affiliate output in Europe rose by around 6% in 2012, while European affiliate output in the U.S. rose by a slightly faster pace, 6.5%. European affiliate output in the U.S. has recovered and expanded since falling to a cyclical low of $391 billion in 2009. U.S. affiliate output in Europe has also recovered from its pre-crisis lows.

We expect further gains in U.S. foreign affiliate output in the near term, supported by Europe's improving economic performance. In the United States, European affiliates are operating in one of the most dynamic developed nations in the world and are expected to boost their near–term output as well.

On a global basis, aggregate output of U.S. foreign affiliates reached $1.6 trillion, with Europe (broadly defined) accounting for around 48% of the total. The latter figure was on par with 2011. The United Kingdom, where U.S. investment ties are deepest, accounted for 22.5% of total affiliate output in Europe in 2012, followed by Ireland (13.8%), and Germany (13.3%). These three nations

accounted for roughly half of total U.S. foreign affiliate output in Europe in 2012, with the largest jump in share gains coming from Ireland.

In 2010, U.S. affiliates in Ireland accounted for roughly 10.3% of total output of European affiliates, although the nation's share rose by over 3 percentage points in the subsequent three years. France's share of affiliate output, in contrast, dropped to 7.7% in 2012 from 8.4% in 2010. By sector, output has been tilting towards services (53%) from manufacturing (47%). Germany, the United Kingdom and Ireland accounted for roughly half of total U.S. affiliate manufacturing output in Europe in 2011, the last year of available data.

The presence of U.S. affiliates in some European countries in particularly notable. The gross output of American affiliates in Ireland, for instance, represented over one-quarter of the country's gross domestic product again in 2012, a staggering contribution on both an absolute and relative basis. This dynamic reflects the large U.S. investment base in Ireland, notably by technology and life science companies. U.S. companies have stuck by Ireland, despite the country's recent economic difficulties. Ireland remains a favorite global destination of U.S. firms and is

TABLE 5: THE U.S. - EUROPEAN EMPLOYMENT BALANCE THOUSANDS OF EMPLOYEES, 2012[1]

Country	European Affiliates of U.S. Companies	U.S. Affiliates of European Companies	Employment Balance
Austria	43.9	14.1	-29.8
Belgium	135.9	165.9	30.1
Denmark	32.7	30.1	-2.7
Finland	21.4	27.3	5.9
France	470.0	531.2	61.2
Germany	644.8	600.5	-44.4
Ireland	103.3	175.0	71.7
Italy	207.8	126.9	-80.9
Luxembourg	14.0	38.0	24.0
Netherlands	228.9	405.0	176.1
Norway	42.1	8.0	-34.1
Spain	177.5	85.0	-92.5
Switzerland	94.6	457.0	362.5
United Kingdom	1,315.3	986.0	-329.4
Europe	**4,275.2**	**3,880.2**	**-395.0**

Note: Employment balance "+" favors the United States
Source: Bureau of Economic Analysis
1. Estimates
Majority-owned bank and non-bank affiliates

the number one export platform in the world for U.S. companies.

Elsewhere, by our estimations, U.S. affiliates accounted for around 6% of the United Kingdom's aggregate output in 2012; 5.8% of Norway's aggregate output; 5% of Switzerland's total output; and 4.9% of Belgium's total output. It is interesting to note that affiliate output in Belgium in 2012 ($25.5 billion) was more than 40% larger than U.S. foreign affiliate output in India (an estimated $18 billion).

In addition to expanding their presence in the more traditional markets of Europe, U.S. firms are taking advantage of the EU's expanding Single Market and incorporating central and eastern European member states, as well as key non-EU countries such as Turkey and Russia, into their European and global production networks. To this point, U.S. affiliate output in Poland rose from $2 billion in 2000 to $12.2 billion in 2011, the last year of available data. We estimate that output rose to $12.6 billion in 2012. Meanwhile, affiliate output in the Czech Republic totaled an estimated $6.1 billion in 2012, after rising from $1.3 billion in 2000 to $5.9 billion in 2011. Between 2000 and 2011, affiliate output in Hungary rose from $1.3 billion to $5 billion, before declining slightly in 2012. U.S. affiliate output in some central and eastern European states now

exceeds output in many smaller developed economies in western Europe.

In the United States, meanwhile, European affiliates are major economic producers in their own right, with British firms of notable importance. The U.S. output of British companies reached $128 billion in 2012, more than a quarter of the European total. For the same year, output from German affiliates operating in the U.S. totaled $87 billion by our estimates, or almost around 18% of the total, while output from French affiliates ($64 billion) accounted for 13% of the total.

Beyond European affiliates, only Corporate Japan and Canada have any real economic presence in the United States. Japanese affiliate output totaled nearly $93 billion in 2011, while Canadian affiliate output totaled $65 billion. Overall, U.S. affiliates of foreign multinationals contributed roughly $775 to U.S. aggregate production in 2012, with European affiliates accounting for roughly two-thirds of the total.

2. Assets of Foreign Affiliates

The global footprint of Corporate America and Corporate Europe is second to none, with each party each other's largest foreign investor. According to the latest data from the Bureau of Labor Statistics, U.S. foreign assets in Europe totaled $12.2 trillion in 2011, representing nearly 60% of the global total.

For 2012, we estimate that U.S. foreign assets in Europe reached $13.2 trillion, close, again, to 60% of the global total. Within the region, the bulk of U.S. assets were in the United Kingdom, with U.S. assets totaling an estimated $5.1 trillion, or 22.5% of the global total.

U.S. assets in the Netherlands (nearly $2 trillion) were the second largest in Europe and in the world in 2012. America's significant presence in the Netherlands reflects its strategic role as an export platform/distribution hub for U.S. firms doing business in the greater European Union. To this point, more than half of affiliate sales in the Netherlands are for export, namely within the EU. Meanwhile, America's asset base in Germany ($721 billion in 2012) was over 50% larger than its asset base in all of South America. America's collective asset base in Poland, the Czech Republic and Hungary (roughly $136 billion) was much larger than corporate America's assts in India (roughly $100 billion). As for Corporate America's in-country presence in Ireland, U.S. assets topped $1 trillion, greater than America's asset base in either Switzerland or France. Ireland accounted for roughly 8.1% of total U.S. assets in Europe in 2011.

As for foreign-owned assets in the United States, Europe's stakes are sizable even after declining after the 2008-09 recession. Total assets of European affiliates in the United States were valued at $8.7 trillion in 2012 by our estimate. The United Kingdom ranked first (est. $2.2 trillion), followed by German firms ($1.5 trillion), Swiss ($1.4 trillion) and French firms ($1.2 trillion). U.S. assets of Dutch firms totaled an estimated $1 trillion in 2012.

3. Affiliate Employment

The outsourcing debate rages on in Washington, with the common assumption that when it comes to hiring workers overseas, the bulk of the hiring is done in low-wage developing nations like Mexico, China and India. Reality is different. Most foreign workers on the payrolls of U.S. foreign affiliates are employed in the developed nations in general, and Europe in particular.

Indeed, between 2000 and 2011, U.S. foreign affiliate employment in Europe rose by 12.9%, increasing from 3.7 million workers in 2000 to 4.2 million in 2011. Figures for 2012 are not yet available but we estimate that the number of workers employed by U.S. affiliates rose to roughly 4.3 million workers. According to estimates, U.S. foreign affiliates added 62,600 new jobs to the UK economy in 2012, created 12,600 new jobs in Germany, 3,500 new jobs in the Czech Republic, 6,700 new jobs in the Netherlands and 1,800 jobs in Spain.

Aggregate employment levels continue to rise but manufacturing employment fell slightly, from 1.9 million at the start of the century to 1.8 million in 2011, the last year of available data. The largest declines in manufacturing employment among U.S. affiliates was reported in the United Kingdom, with the total manufacturing work force declining to 301,000 in 2011 from 431,000 in 2000. Employment in France dropped from 249,000 to 199,000, and a decline from 388,000 to 359,000 was recorded in Germany, although there was a net gain of U.S. affiliate employment in Germany of 5,500 in 2011 from 2010. Poland was a big gainer: U.S. affiliate employment there doubled between 2000 and 2011, climbing from 51,000 to over 100,000 in 2011.

On a global basis, U.S. majority-owned affiliates (banks and non-banks) employed roughly 11.8 million workers in 2012, with the bulk of these workers—roughly 35%—toiling in Europe. That share is down from 41% in 2008. The decline is due in part to the cyclical fall in output and employment across recession-weary Europe. It also reflects the fact that a rising share of U.S. overseas capacity (manufacturing and services) is expanding at a faster pace in the high-growth emerging markets versus slow-growth developed nations.

The bulk of affiliate employees in Europe are based in the United Kingdom, Germany and France, a trend little changed from previous years. What is changing, however, is that U.S. majority-owned foreign affiliates are on balance hiring more people in the services sector than in manufacturing.

Manufacturing employment accounted for just 42.5% of total employment in 2011, the last year of available data. The top industry in terms of manufacturing employment was transportation, with U.S. affiliates employing nearly 373,000 workers, followed by chemicals (264,000). Wholesale employment was among the largest sources of services-related employment, which includes employment in such areas as logistics, trade, insurance and other related activities.

Although services employment among U.S. affiliate has grown at a faster pace than manufacturing employment over the past decade, it is interesting to note that U.S. affiliates employed more manufacturing workers in Europe in 2011 (1.8 million) than in 1990 (1.6 million).

However, while the aggregate number of U.S. manufacturing jobs in Europe has increased, the geographic distribution of such jobs has shifted over the past few decades. In general, the shift has been towards lower cost locations like Ireland, Poland and Hungary, at the expense of the United Kingdom, France and Germany. To this point, the later three nations accounted for 67% of total U.S. affiliate manufacturing employment in Europe in 1990. In 2011, their share had been reduced to 48.3%. The United Kingdom took the biggest hit, with the UK's share of U.S. affiliate manufacturing employment accounting for just 17% of the total in 2011, versus a share of 29% in 1990. Between 1990 and 2011, U.S. affiliate manufacturing employment in the United Kingdom and Germany fell by roughly 35% and 10%, respectively. Meanwhile, manufacturing employment in Ireland soared by over 40% over the same period, while the combined share of U.S. affiliate manufacturing employment in Poland, the Czech Republic and Hungary jumped from virtually zero to nearly 11% in 2011, indicative of the eastern spread of U.S. European operations.

Even given these changes, the manufacturing workforce of U.S. affiliates in Germany totaled nearly 360,000 workers in 2011—above the number of manufactured workers employed in Brazil (316,000), and India (149,000) yet below the figures from China (574,000).

When it comes to affiliate employment, trends in the United States are similar to those in Europe. In other words, despite stories on the continent about local European companies decamping for cheap labor markets in central Europe or Asia, most foreigners working for European firms outside of Europe are Americans. Based on the latest figures, European majority-owned foreign affiliates directly employed roughly 3.9 million U.S. workers in 2012—some 400,000 less workers than U.S. affiliates employed in Europe. By our estimates, the top five European employers in the U.S. were firms from the United Kingdom (986,000), Germany (600,000), France, (531,000), Switzerland (457,000), and the Netherlands (405,000). European firms employed roughly two-thirds of all U.S. workers on the payrolls of majority-owned foreign affiliates in 2012.

According to estimates, UK affiliates created 42,500 new U.S. jobs in 2012, Dutch companies generated an additional 5,200 jobs, Italian companies 6,200 more, Irish companies 8,100 more, and French companies in the U.S. generated an additional 6,800 jobs. Swiss companies employed an additional 10,700 people in the United States, German companies an extra 19,200 and Spanish companies 3,600 new U.S. jobs.

In the aggregate, the transatlantic workforce directly employed by U.S. and European foreign affiliates in 2011 was roughly 8.2 million strong, up roughly 3% from the prior year. In 2013, modest gains in employment were most likely achieved as employment rebounded due to increased hiring among European firms based in the United States. That said, as we have stressed in the past, these figures understate the employment effects of mutual investment flows, since these numbers are limited to direct employment, and do not account for indirect employment effects on nonequity arrangements such as strategic alliances, joint ventures, and other deals. Moreover, affiliate employment figures do not include jobs supported by transatlantic trade flows. Trade-related employment is substantial in many U.S. states and many European regions.

In total, and adding indirect employment, we estimate that the transatlantic work force numbers some 13-15 million workers. Europe is by far the most important source of "onshored" jobs in America, and the U.S. is by far the most important source of "onshored" jobs in Europe.

4. Research and Development of Foreign Affiliates

The globalization of R&D has gathered pace over the past decade, with more and more global R&D expenditures emanating from China, South Korea, and Japan—or Asia in general. There are no boundaries to innovation thanks to proliferation of the internet and falling global communications. Both dynamics have helped spawn more R&D from the developing nations; indeed, based on the rankings of the top ten R&D-spending nations in 2014, the rankings were evenly split between developed nations and developing nations.

The United States ranked first, followed by China, Japan, Germany, South Korea, France, the United Kingdom, India, Russia and Brazil. Four of the top ten nations were transatlantic economies; four were also the BRICs—Brazil, Russia, India and China, underscoring the fact that R&D is no longer the sole preserve of the developed nations.

The figures come from the *2014 Global R&D Funding Forecast*, produced by Battelle and *R&D Magazine*. As the report notes:

» In 2014, ten countries will spend more than 80% of the total $1.6 trillion invested on R&D around the world; the combined investment by the U.S., China, and Japan will account for more than half, and with Europe about 78%, of the total.

» Given the current, weak economic environment in Europe, large increases in R&D investments are not expected for the next several years.

» The United States remains the world's largest R&D investor with projected $465 billion spending in 2014.

» At the current rates of growth and investment, China's total funding of R&D is expected to surpass that of the U.S. by about 2022.

While governments and corporations are the main generators of R&D spending, foreign affiliates of multinationals are also in the thick of things. Indeed, foreign affiliate R&D has become more prominent over the past decades as firms seek to share development costs, spread risks and tap into the intellectual talent of other nations. Alliances, cross-licensing of intellectual property, mergers and acquisition, and other forms cooperation have become more prevalent characteristics of the transatlantic economy in the past decade. The internet, in particular, has powered greater transatlantic R&D. The complexity of scientific and technological innovation is leading innovators to partner and share costs, find complementary expertise, gain access to different technologies and knowledge quickly, and collaborate as part of "open" innovation networks. Cross-border collaboration with foreign partners can range from a simple one-way transmission of information to highly interactive and formal arrangements. Developing new products, creating new processes and driving more innovation—all of the above results from more collaboration between foreign suppliers and U.S. and European companies.

TABLE 6: THE INNOVATION TOP 20

Rank 2011	Company	R & D Spending 2013, $US Billions	Change from 2012	Headquarters Location	Industry
1	Volkswagen	11.4	22.4%	Germany	Auto
2	Samsung	10.4	15.6%	South Korea	Computing and Electronics
3	Roche Holding	10.2	14.7%	Switzerland	Healthcare
4	Intel	10.1	21.5%	U.S.	Computing and Electronics
5	Microsoft	9.8	8.5%	U.S.	Software and Internet
6	Toyota	9.8	3.5%	Japan	Auto
7	Novartis	9.3	-2.6%	Switzerland	Healthcare
8	Merck	8.2	-3.5%	U.S.	Healthcare
9	Pfizer	7.9	-13.3%	U.S.	Healthcare
10	Johnson & Johnson	7.7	1.6%	U.S.	Healthcare
11	General Motors	7.4	-9.3%	U.S.	Auto
12	Google	6.8	31.6%	U.S.	Software and Internet
13	Honda	6.8	7.8%	Japan	Auto
14	Daimler	6.6	3.2%	Germany	Auto
15	Sanofi	6.3	2.3%	France	Healthcare
16	IBM	6.3	0.7%	U.S.	Computing and Electronics
17	GlaxoSmithKline	6.3	-1.0%	United Kingdom	Healthcare
18	Nokia	6.1	-14.4%	Finland	Computing and Electronics
19	Panasonic	6.1	-3.5%	Japan	Computing and Electronics
20	Sony	5.7	9.3%	Japan	Computing and Electronics
	Top 20 Total	**159.2**	**8.1%**		

Source: Booz & Company

Bilateral U.S.-EU flows in R&D are the most intense between any two international partners. In 2011, the last year of available data, U.S. affiliates sunk $27.7 billion on research and development in Europe, an increase of $3.3 billion over 2010 and roughly 61% of the total R&D expenditures of total global R&D by U.S. foreign affiliates of $45.7 billion. R&D expenditures by U.S. affiliates were greatest in Germany, the United Kingdom, Switzerland, France, the Netherlands, Belgium and Ireland. These seven nations accounted for 86% of U.S. global spending on R&D in Europe in 2011.

In the United States, meanwhile, expenditures on R&D performed by majority-owned foreign affiliates totaled $45.2 billion in 2011, up around 7% from the prior year. As

in previous years, a significant share of this R&D spending emanated from world-class leaders from Europe, given their interest in America's highly skilled labor force and first-class university infrastructure. Most of this investment took place among European firms in such research-intensive sectors as autos, energy, chemicals, and telecommunications. In 2011, R&D spending by European affiliates totaled $33.4 billion, over $2 billion more than in 2010 and a sizable high value-added capital investment representing three-fourths of all R&D performed by majority-owned foreign affiliates in the United States.

By country, Swiss-owned affiliates were the largest foreign source of R&D in the U.S. in 2011; Swiss-owned R&D in the

TABLE 7: RELATED PARTY TRADE, 2012

	US Imports: "Related Party Trade," as % of Total	US Exports: "Related Party Trade," as % of Total
European Union	61.8	32.2
Germany	69.2	34.9
France	52.4	28.3
Ireland	89.9	30.7
Netherlands	64.8	45.4
United Kingdom	54.9	27.9

Source: U.S. Census Bureau

U.S. totaled $8.9 billion, down slightly from $9.3 billion the year before. Swiss firms accounted for nearly one-fifth of total affiliate R&D in the United States. British affiliates accounted for the second largest percentage of affiliate expenditures, with a 14.2% share in 2011. The share of Germany and France was 12.2% and 11.1%, respectively.

As Table 6 underscores, some of the world's most innovative companies are domiciled in the United States and Europe.

5. Intra-Firm Trade of Foreign Affiliates

While cross-border trade is a secondary means of delivery goods and services across the Atlantic, the modes of delivery—affiliate sales and trade—should not be viewed independently. They are more complements than substitutes, since foreign investment and affiliate sales increasingly drive cross-border trade flows. Indeed, a substantial share of transatlantic trade is considered intra-firm trade or related-party trade, which is cross-border trade that stays within the ambit of the company. Intra-firm or related-party trade occurs when BMW or Mercedes of Germany send parts to BMW of South Carolina or Mercedes of Alabama; when Lafarge or Michelin send intermediate components to their plants in the Greater Cincinnati area, or when 3M ships components for its office products or communications sectors from St. Paul to affiliates in Germany or the UK.

The tight linkages between European parent companies and their U.S. affiliates are reflected in the fact that roughly 62% of U.S. imports from the European Union consisted of related-party trade in 2012. That is much higher than the related party imports from the Pacific Rim nations (43.3%) and South/Central America (39.5%), and well above the global average (50.3%). The percentage was even higher in the case of Ireland (89.9%) and Germany (69.2%).

Meanwhile, roughly one-third (32.3%) of U.S. exports to Europe in 2012 represented related-party trade, but the percentage is higher for some countries. For instance, almost half of total U.S. exports to Belgium (49.5%) and the Netherlands in 2012 (45.4%) was classified as related-party trade. The comparable figure for Germany was 34.9% and 27.9% for the United Kingdom.

6. Foreign Affiliate Sales

U.S. majority-owned foreign affiliate sales on a global basis (goods and services) totaled an estimated $6.6 trillion in 2012, having rebounded from the decline in 2009 caused by the global recession. Total U.S. exports, in contrast, were $2.2 trillion in 2012—a sizable difference that underscores the primacy of foreign affiliate sales over U.S. exports. One of the best kept secrets in Washington is how U.S. firms actually deliver goods and services to foreign customers.

As usual, Europe accounted for the bulk of U.S. affiliate sales in 2012. We estimate that U.S. foreign affiliate sales in Europe topped $3 trillion for the first time, rising roughly 8% from the prior year. U.S. affiliate sales in Europe amounted to nearly 47% of the global total.

Reflecting just how important Europe is to Corporate America, sales of U.S. affiliates in Europe in 2011, the last year of available data, were roughly double comparable sales in the entire Asia/Pacific region. Affiliate sales in the United Kingdom ($665 billion) were almost double aggregate sales to South America. Sales in Germany ($352 billion) were 80% larger than combined sales in Africa and the Middle East. While U.S. affiliate sales in China have soared over the past decade, they have done so from a low base, and still remain well below comparable sales in Europe. For instance, U.S. affiliate sales of $206 billion in China in 2011 were below those in France ($220 billion), the Netherlands ($228 billion) and Switzerland ($304 billion). U.S. foreign affiliate sales in Ireland ranked third in Europe at $320 billion in 2011—a good share of these sales, however, take the form of U.S. affiliate exports to the EU and other third markets.

Affiliate sales are also the primary means by which European firms deliver goods and services to consumers in the United States. In 2012, for instance, we estimate that majority-owned European affiliate sales in the United States ($2.2 trillion) were more than triple U.S. imports from Europe (roughly $655 billion). Affiliate sales rose by roughly 6% in 2012, by our estimate. By country, sales of British firms led the way, totaling an estimated $521 billion in 2012—$27 billion more than in 2011—followed by Germany ($411 billion) and the Netherlands ($374 billion). For virtually all countries in Europe, foreign affiliate sales were easily in excess of their U.S. imports in 2011.

TABLE 8: U.S. EARNINGS FROM EUROPE HITTING NEW HIGHS (U.S. FOREIGN AFFILIATE INCOME FROM EUROPE)

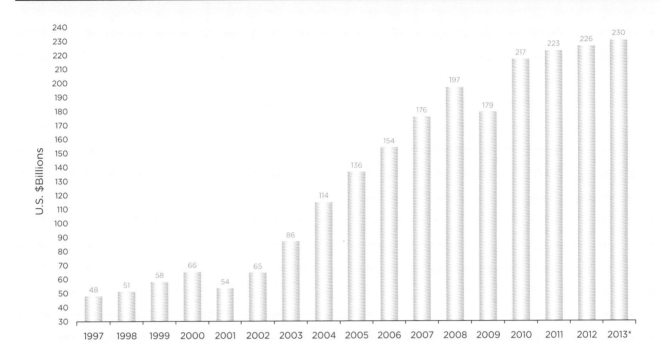

Source: Bureau of Economic Analysis
* Data through 3Q2013. Data annualized for full year estimate

7. Foreign Affiliate Profits

After plunging in 2009, transatlantic affiliate profits rebounded in 2010 and have continued to increase, albeit moderately in some cases, to the current day. Looking just at 2012, U.S. affiliate income in Europe inched up to $226.4 billion from $223 billion the year before. In the first nine months of 2013, U.S. affiliate income totaled $172.2 billion, up slightly from the same period a year earlier. In the aggregate, income rose very modestly in 2013, by less than 2% by our estimate, to $230 billion. The slight rise represents an all-time high for what U.S. affiliates earned in Europe, yet masks deep declines over many parts of Europe.

The general weakness in U.S. affiliate income in Europe was widespread—for instance, affiliate income in France and Germany in the January-September 2013 period was down 12% and 63%, respectively, from the same period a year earlier. Income fell 144% in Greece and 65% in Italy over the same period. U.S. affiliate income in Spain plunged 25%. On the positive side, affiliate income in the January-September period was up a 8% in Switzerland (year over year), and rose 12.8% in the UK and 1.1% in Ireland. Without these strong gains, U.S. affiliate income would have declined for the year.

In 2014, we expect a continued gradual improvement among U.S. foreign affiliates in Europe. Affiliate earnings

weakened over the second half of 2011 as the European debt crisis triggered widening credit spreads, a contraction in lending, a drop in consumer and business confidence, and pushed many parts of Europe into recession. Europe limped into 2013 but gained strength as the year wore on. The situation is likely to improve moderately as this year progresses.

Despite a very soft earnings backdrop for U.S. affiliates in Europe in 2013, the region still accounted for slightly more than half (52%) of global foreign affiliate income for the first three quarters of the year. Hence, Europe remains an important market to U.S. firms. Indeed, since 2000, Europe has accounted for over 57% of total U.S. foreign affiliate income. As a footnote, we define Europe here in very broad terms, including not only the EU28, but also Norway, Switzerland, Russia and smaller markets in central and eastern Europe. See our endnotes for the exact definition.

On a comparative basis, U.S. affiliate income from Europe is simply staggering, with foreign affiliate income in Europe—$172 billion in the first nine months of 2013—more than the combined affiliate income of Latin America ($64 billion) and Asia ($56 billion). It is interesting to note that combined U.S. affiliate income from China and India in 2012 ($10.4 billion) was only around 15% of what U.S. affiliates

TABLE 9: U.S. - EUROPE SERVICE LINKAGES

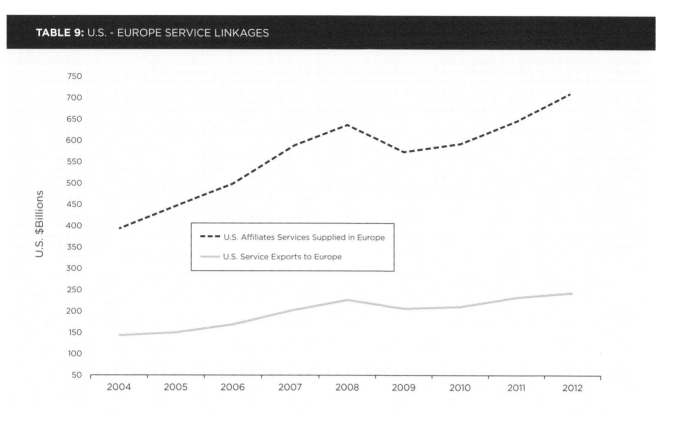

Source: Bureau of Economic Analysis
Majority-owned bank and non-bank affiliates. Services Supplied in Europe estimate for 2012.

earned/reported in the Netherlands ($73 billion) and a fraction of U.S. affiliate earnings in the United Kingdom ($36 billion) or Ireland ($30 billion). These trends continued into 2013; U.S. affiliate income in Ireland between January-September 2013 of $23.2 billion was more than three times U.S. affiliate income from China ($7 billion).

Still, there is little doubt that the likes of India, Brazil and China are becoming more important earnings engines for U.S. firms. To this point, in the first nine months of 2013, U.S. affiliate income of $7 billion in China alone was well in excess of affiliate income in Germany ($1.1 billion), France ($2.2 billion) and Spain (only $265 million - down from $1.9 billion in the same period in 2012). U.S. affiliates in Brazil earned nearly $5.7 billion in the January-September period, less than the same period a year earlier yet well more than that earned in many European nations.

All of that said, we see rising U.S. affiliate earnings from the emerging markets as a complement, not a substitute, to earnings from Europe. The latter very much remains a key source of prosperity for corporate America.

Similarly, the United States remains the most important market in the world in terms of earnings for many European multinationals. Profits of European affiliates in the United States plunged 21.3% in 2009, soared in 2010—by 22.3%—and 2011 before leveling off in 2012. A slight decline was posted in 2013. In the first nine months of 2013, the income of European affiliates dropped 5.4% from the same period a year earlier. For all of 2013, we estimate European affiliate income in the U.S. fell by roughly 5%, to $119 billion, with the decline reflecting subpar growth in the U.S. and the stronger euro against the dollar, which reduced affiliates' dollar-based earnings in the United States.

8. Transatlantic Services Linkages

Services are the sleeping giant of the transatlantic economy—a key area offering significant opportunities for stronger and deeper transatlantic commercial ties.[1]

The United States and Europe are the two leading services economies in the world. According to the World Trade Organization, the U.S. is the largest single country trader in services, while the EU is the largest trader in services among all world regions, accounting for 46.7% of global exports of services. Among the three largest components of global services trade—travel, transportation and other commercial services—Europe ranks number one in each category. However, exports of services from Europe declined by 2.3% in 2012 owing to depressed economic conditions in the region. According to the World Trade

TABLE 10: EUROPE - U.S. SERVICE LINKAGES

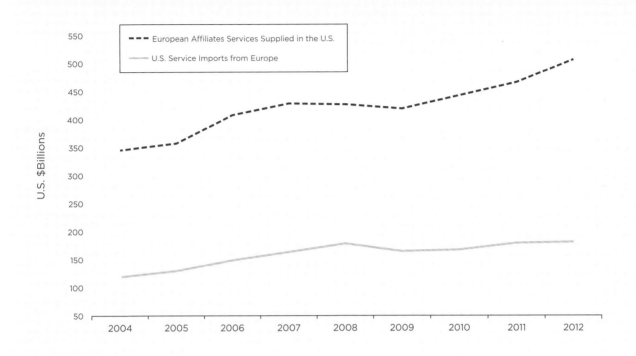

Source: Bureau of Economic Analysis
Majority-owned bank and non-bank affiliates. Services Supplied in the U.S. estimate for 2012.

Organization, the UK, the world's largest services exporter after the United States, saw exports decline by 3.4% in 2012; Germany's services exports declined by 1.1%, while France's services exports dropped 5.7%. Services exports from the United States, in contrast, rose 5.5% in 2012.

Transatlantic services trade figures are impressive. But the more important services linkages are actually in mutual flows of foreign direct investment. The services economies of the United States and Europe have become even more intertwined over the past year, with cross-border trade in services and sales through affiliates posting strong gains. By sectors, transatlantic linkages continue to deepen in financial services, insurance, education, telecommunications, utilities, advertising, and computer services. Other sectors such as aviation and e-health are slowly being liberalized and deregulated.

On a regional basis, Europe accounted for 38.1% of total U.S. services exports and for 41.6% of total U.S. services imports in 2012. Five out of the top ten export markets for U.S. services in 2012 were in Europe. The United Kingdom ranked #2, followed by Ireland (5th), Germany (7th), Switzerland (8th) and France (10th). Similarly, four of the countries just mentioned were among the top ten services providers to the U.S. The United Kingdom ranked #1,

followed by Germany (5th), Switzerland (6th), and France (9th).[2] The U.S. enjoyed a $66.8 billion trade surplus in services with Europe in 2012, compared with its $126 billion trade deficit in goods with Europe.

Thanks to a variety of factors—stronger growth, the weaker dollar, EU enlargement, industry reform and deregulation— U.S. services exports to Europe more than doubled between 2001 and 2012, rising from around $102 billion to $239 billion. U.S. services exports to Europe plunged by 9.4% in 2009 but rose 2.6% in 2010, 10.7% in 2011, and 3.8% in 2012, helped by rising exports (or receipts) of a number of services-related items like travel, passenger fares, and royalties and license fees. Gains were also reported among exports of "other private services," or in such value-added activities as computer processing, engineering, advertising and related activities. In this category, U.S. exports to Europe totaled $116 billion in 2012, yielding a near $30 billion trade surplus.

U.S. private services imports from Europe, meanwhile, also rebounded in 2012, rising 3.2% from the prior year. Services imports peaked at $167.1 billion in 2008, more than double the levels of 1999, before reaching a new peak last year at $172 billion. The same top countries that ranked in the top ten U.S. services export markets also ranked among the top ten services providers to the U.S. (Ireland ranked 11ᵗʰ). On a regional basis, Europe accounted for just roughly 42% of total U.S. services imports in 2012.

Meanwhile, while the U.S. recorded a $116 billion deficit in goods exports with the European Union in 2012, a sizable amount of the deficit in goods was offset by America's $56 billion surplus in private services. That was up from a surplus of roughly $54 billion in 2012. The U.S. enjoyed a sizable surplus in many activities, including financial services, travel and in particular in "other private services," notably in activities associated with "business, professional and technical services." The latter surplus was roughly $12 billion in 2012. By activity, the U.S. registered a surplus in computer and information services, management consulting, legal services, construction engineering, and operational leasing with Europe in 2012. Top U.S. business services exports to Europe included management, consulting, and public relations services ($20.2 billion in 2012), research, development, and testing services ($17.9 billion); and computer and information services ($9.1 billion).

Beyond services trade, there are the foreign affiliate sales of services, or the delivery of transatlantic services by U.S. and European foreign affiliates. Sales of affiliates have exploded on both sides of the Atlantic over the past decade; indeed, affiliate sales of services have not only supplemented trade in services but also become the overwhelming mode of delivery in a rather short period of time. Affiliate sales of U.S. services rose more than 10-fold between 1990 and 2011, topping $1 trillion for the first time in 2007. In the same year, U.S. services exports were roughly half the level of affiliate sales of services.

Not unexpectedly, and reflecting the transatlantic recession, sales of services of U.S. foreign affiliates in Europe declined in 2009 but have rebounded since then in 2011, the last year of available data. Sales rose to $645 billion in 2011, up from $571 billion in 2009. Notwithstanding this modest rise, sales of services by U.S. affiliates in Europe were more than two and half times U.S. services exports to Europe in 2011. The United Kingdom accounted for around 30% of all U.S. affiliate sales in Europe; UK services sales totaled $191 billion in 2011, an increase of 1% from the prior year but nevertheless greater than total affiliate sales of services in South and Central America

TABLE 11: AMERICA'S FDI ROOTS IN EUROPE (BILLIONS OF $)

Industry	US FDI to Europe	% of Industry Total
European Total	2,477	56%
Manufacturing	311	49%

TABLE 12: EUROPE'S FDI ROOTS IN THE US (BILLIONS OF $)

Industry	US FDI from Europe	% of Industry Total
Total from Europe	1,876	71%
Manufacturing	718	80%

Note: Historic-cost basis, 2011
Source: Bureau of Economic Analysis

($111 billion), Africa ($13 billion) and the Middle East ($29 billion). On a global basis, Europe accounted for 50% of total U.S. services sales.

U.S. affiliate sales of services in the EU continue to exceed sales of services by U.S. affiliates of European firms. The latter totaled $467 billion in 2011, the former some $645 billion. However, on a country-by-country basis, French and German affiliates sold more services in the U.S. in 2011 than American affiliates sold in France and Germany. Of particular note, European affiliate sales of services were more than two and a half times larger than U.S. services imports—a fact that underscores the ever-widening presence of European services leaders in the U.S. economy.

In fact, the U.S. and EU each owe a good part of their competitive position in services globally to deep transatlantic connections in services industries provided by mutual investment flows. A good share of U.S. services exports to the world are generated by European companies based in the United States, just as a good share of EU services exports to the world are generated by U.S. companies based in Europe.

In the end, these eight indices convey a more complete and complex picture of global engagement than simple tallies of exports and imports. Foreign direct investment and foreign affiliate sales, not trade, represent the backbone of the transatlantic economy. The eight variables just highlighted underscore the depth and breadth of the transatlantic commercial relationship.

Endnotes

1. For a closer examination of the transatlantic services economy, see Daniel S. Hamilton and Joseph P. Quinlan, eds., *Sleeping Giant: Awakening the Transatlantic Services Economy* (Washington, DC: Center for Transatlantic Relations, 2007).
2. Bureau of Economic Analysis, U.S. International Services, Cross-Border Services Exports and Imports by Type and Country.

Notes on Terms, Data and Sources

EMPLOYMENT, INVESTMENT, AND TRADE LINKAGES FOR THE 50 U.S. STATES AND EUROPE
Data for investment as well as investment-related jobs are from the U.S. Commerce Department's Bureau of Economic Analysis. Investment data measure gross property, plant, and equipment of affiliates. Europe includes Belgium, France, Germany, Italy, Netherlands, Sweden, Switzerland, and the United Kingdom. Trade data are from the International Trade Administration's Office of Trade and Industry Information at the U.S. Commerce Department. Europe includes Albania, Andorra, Armenia, Austria, Azerbaijan, Belarus, Belgium, Bosnia-Herzegovina, Bulgaria, Croatia, Czech Republic, Cyprus, Denmark, Estonia, Faeroe Islands, Finland, France, Germany, Georgia, Gibraltar, Greece, Iceland, Ireland, Italy, Latvia, Liechtenstein, Lithuania, Luxembourg, Macedonia, Malta, Moldova, Monaco, Montenegro, Netherlands, Norway, Poland, Portugal, Romania, Russia, San Marino, Serbia, Slovakia, Slovenia, Spain, Svalbard, Sweden, Switzerland, Tajikistan, Turkey, Ukraine, United Kingdom, Vatican City. The top ten exports to Europe bar chart employs a logarithmic scale to facilitate cross state comparisons.

INVESTMENT AND TRADE FOR THE EU 28, NORWAY, SWITZERLAND, TURKEY AND THE U.S.
Investment data are from the Bureau of Economic Analysis. Trade data are from the IMF Trade Statistics. Data for the top ten U.S. imports bar charts are from the Office of Trade and Industry Information of the International Trade Administration. They employ logarithmic scales to facilitate cross-country comparisons.

TERMS
Throughout this report, the term "EU" refers to all 28 member states of the European Union. The term EU15 refers to the older EU member states: the United Kingdom, Ireland, Belgium, Luxembourg, the Netherlands, Austria, Spain, Italy, Greece, France, Germany, Portugal, Sweden, Finland, and Denmark. The term EU12 refers to the newer EU member states: Estonia, Latvia, Lithuania, Poland, the Czech Republic, Slovakia, Hungary, Slovenia, Malta, Cyprus, Romania and Bulgaria. EU12 data does not include Croatia, which on July 1, 2013 became the 28th member state of the European Union.

In addition to the above, the term "Europe" in this report refers to the following: all 28 members of the European Union plus Russia, Turkey, Switzerland, Albania, Andorra, Armenia, Azerbaijan, Belarus, Bosnia and Herzegovina, Georgia, Gibraltar, Greenland, Iceland, Kazakhstan, Kyrgyzstan, Macedonia, Malta, Moldova, Monaco, Montenegro, Serbia, Tajikistan, Turkmenistan, Union of Soviet Socialist Republics, Uzbekistan.

About the Authors

DANIEL S. HAMILTON and **JOSEPH P. QUINLAN** have been producing *The Transatlantic Economy* annual survey since 2004. They have authored and edited a series of award-winning books and articles on the modern transatlantic economy, including *Atlantic Rising: Changing Commercial Dynamics in the Atlantic Basin* (2014); *Germany and Globalization* (2009); *France and Globalization* (2009); *Globalization and Europe: Prospering in a New Whirled Order* (2008); *Sleeping Giant: Awakening the Transatlantic Services Economy* (2007); *Protecting Our Prosperity: Ensuring Both National Security and the Benefits of Foreign Investment in the United States* (2006); *Deep Integration: How Transatlantic Markets are Leading Globalization* (2005); and *Partners in Prosperity: The Changing Geography of the Transatlantic Economy* (2004). Together they were recipients of the 2007 Transatlantic Leadership Award by the European-American Business Council and the 2006 Transatlantic Business Award by the American Chamber of Commerce to the European Union.

DANIEL S. HAMILTON is the Austrian Marshall Plan Foundation Professor and Director of the Center for Transatlantic Relations at the Paul H. Nitze School of Advanced International Studies, Johns Hopkins University. He also serves as Executive Director of the American Consortium on EU Studies, designated by the European Commission as the EU Center of Excellence Washington, DC. He has been a consultant for Microsoft and an advisor to the U.S. Business Roundtable, the Transatlantic Business Dialogue, and the European-American Business Council. Recent books include *Open Ukraine: Changing Course towards a European Future; Europe's Economic Crisis*, co-edited with Nobel Prize Laureate Robert Solow; *Transatlantic 2020: A Tale of Four Futures*, and *Europe 2020: Competitive or Complacent?* He has served in a variety of senior positions in the U.S. State Department, including as Deputy Assistant Secretary of State.

JOSEPH P. QUINLAN is Senior Fellow at the Center for Transatlantic Relations, with extensive experience in the U.S. corporate sector. He is a leading expert on the transatlantic economy and well-known global economist/strategist on Wall Street. He specializes in global capital flows, international trade and multinational strategies. He lectures at New York University, and his publications have appeared in such venues as *Foreign Affairs*, the *Financial Times* and the *Wall Street Journal*. His recent book is *The Last Economic Superpower: The Retreat of Globalization, the End of American Dominance, and What We Can Do About It* (New York: McGraw Hill, 2010).